The Cheshire Lines Railway between

Glazebrook and Godley

A route of strategic importance

Bob Pixton

Kestrel Railway Books
PO Box 269
SOUTHAMPTON
SO30 4XR

www.kestrelrailwaybooks.co.uk

Printed by The Amadeus Press

ISBN 978-1-905505-21-0

Front cover: A down train passes on the original line down from Skelton Junction to meet the MSJ&AR at Deansgate Junction. Stanier 8F 2-8-0 No 48390 probably collected its trainload of hopper wagons from the limestone quarries of the Peak District, and will deliver them to the vast chemical works west of Winsford. *(Colour-Rail)*

Back cover (top): The footplate crew of Stanier 8F 2-8-0 No 48503 await their next job under the wires at Godley Junction on 26th March 1966. From the early 1950s, steam trains handed empties to electric trains here for their journey through the Pennines to Wath or Rotherwood. Loaded wagons from those places would be steam-hauled from here to south Lancashire, much of the traffic destined for the docks at Liverpool or the coal basin at Partington. *(Geoff Plumb)*

Back cover (bottom): Languishing in the bay at Stockport Tiviot Dale on a rainy 26th March 1966 is Ivatt 2-6-0 No 43063. Eastbound trains frequently needed assistance up the gradient towards Woodley Junction, and engines such as this one would buffer up behind a passing train to provide much-needed help. They would then return as a light engine to sit here and await their next turn. *(Geoff Plumb)*

Title Page: Almost fifty years ago this would have been the scene – the buildings are still here today. Heading west through Glazebrook on 20th June 1964 is Stanier 2-8-0 No 48338 with a fitted breakdown train. The rear wagons are passing under Glazebrook Lane bridge. On the up line, the signals for East Junction show up well with the line to Skelton Junction diverging half a mile distant. Ahead of the train is Dam Lane and West Junction. *(Clive IK Field)*

The Cheshire Lines Railway between

Glazebrook and Godley

A route of strategic importance

Introduction

The railway line between Glazebrook and Godley has an importance that exceeds both the towns it serves and its length. Crossing mostly through rural Cheshire, the passenger service was modest at its best, with Stockport the only major town along its route. Here, the line seems to play second fiddle to the LNWR up on the viaduct and at Edgeley station. This short, Cheshire, line, just under nineteen miles in length, has two sections of quadruple track, so why was it so important?

As the cockpit of the Industrial Revolution, Manchester, soon developed an impressive railway system. This brought in everything that the factories needed, and transported all the finished products to distant markets. However, its radiating lines were a barrier to trainloads of goods not needing to go there, for example, from Derbyshire and Yorkshire to and from Liverpool. The Glazebrook to Godley line was developed as a means of bypassing Manchester for such goods – so much so that it became one of the most intensively-used freight sections of track in the country.

The railway companies developed their own marshalling yards around the east of the city to separate traffic for this line at Gowhole (MR), Mottram (GCR), Dewsnap sidings (GCR), and at Edgeley and Jubilee sidings (LNWR). The corresponding features in the west were at Warrington, Halewood and Liverpool with its docks. Birkenhead and its docks were also accessed via the Cheshire Lines system. Excursion trains used it extensively, utilizing its strategic links at either end, and enabling people from Yorkshire, Nottinghamshire and Derbyshire to access the Lake District, Lancashire coast and North Wales without having to pass through Manchester. Other recreation sites such as race meetings at Chester, Aintree and Haydock Park also used the lines to avoid Manchester.

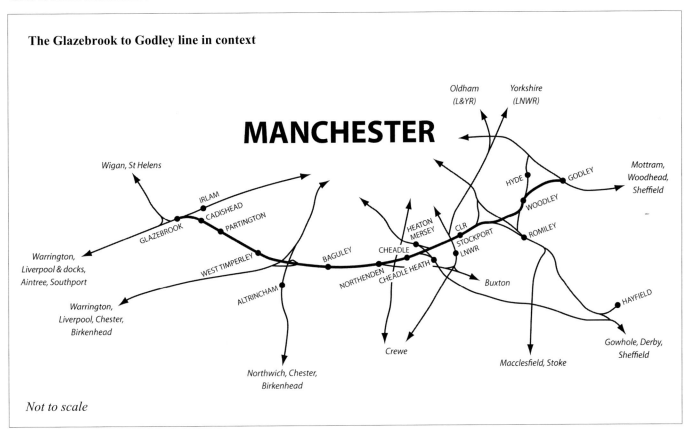

The Glazebrook to Godley line in context

Not to scale

It was the desire to avoid the city of Manchester that led to the building of the Cheshire Lines Railway, which comprised several relatively short pieces of line that linked other lines. It is perhaps hard for us to appreciate the mass movement of goods in an era before the lorry-dominated road transport of today, hence the importance of this railway.

One great flow was coal. At its peak in 1913, something like 287 million tons was mined – four times as much as today, indeed, we exported approximately the total amount mined today! Over a third was used for bunkers of ships and a quarter for export, with 13.5 million tons being used by steam engines themselves (almost 5% of the total).

Before the Great War, the British Royal Navy and merchant fleets were the biggest in the world, and all were powered by steam; *Lusitania* and *Mauritania* used 1,000 tons of coal per day on trans-Atlantic crossings. All this, with less-efficient steam engines, marshalling yards, every home burning domestic coal and every town having its town gas plant, resulted in a vast industry. And on top of the traffic generated there were also the returning empty wagons!

In addition were holidays and day trips to the seaside, and all were achieved by train. However, business alters, and so must the railways that serve it. The decline in coal used in homes, domestically by railways, by ships and for export, together with the contraction in the iron and steel industry, removed some of the bigger users from the railway. Holiday makers' preference for motorways and airports has all but eliminated the holiday excursion train, so deprived of its biggest customers, some sections of the line are now closed while others still carry passenger trains.

Great Rocks Junction, around 1960. Featured frequently in this account are the celebrated "Hopper Trains". Each 22-ton wagon takes around 43.5 tons of crushed limestone from here to Northwich in Cheshire. There, in a chemical reaction with locally-mined salt, crude sodium carbonate is made – a chemical building block for many other substances using the Solvay process. This block train idea was developed in the late 1930s, and when 8F engines became available, a rake of 16 became the standard train. The 1966 working timetable shows eight such trains each day, and as seen here, the resulting empties. Stanier 2-8-0 48605 has been given the right to proceed by the small arm on the bracket signal above the fifth wagon being operated by lever no 34 in the signalbox we are standing in. The engine is taking its train onto the down main, and will continue into the sidings, where, the two will separate, industrial saddle tanks taking charge of the wagons for refilling. After reversing to the up side, the engine will be serviced and turned, and will then be ready to collect another train of over 1,000 tons. Its route will be along the Midland line to join our route north of Cheadle Heath. Passing west to Skelton Junction it will then gain access to the Cheshire Lines route to Northwich. This limestone traffic from Derbyshire to Northwich in Cheshire is a 5 million-ton-per-year dinosaur that still reflects the line's former glories. *(CM & JM Bentley)*

The Cheshire Lines Railway Around Glazebrook and its Junctions

As its name suggests, Glazebrook is close to the River Glaze, one of the rivers that drains the infamous Chat Moss into the River Mersey. This is an area of 25-30 square miles of very poorly draining land due to the impervious clay bed some twenty feet below. Fifty years before this line was built, surveys were done for the original Liverpool to Manchester Railway. At that time, it was deemed a wasteland to be avoided, and a barrier that needed detours to get round it. However, when the L&M was built in the late 1820s, it was decided to let the railway line "float" on the moss by covering it with brushwood, and adding cinders and soil. This was repeated until a stable trackbed was achieved. While this line is some three miles to the south of the L&M line, it passes over the edges of the Moss, so similar difficulties would have had to be overcome.

Until 1873, the newly-formed Cheshire Lines Railway's trains from Manchester to Liverpool had to pass on lines operated jointly with (for example) the Manchester South Junction & Altrincham Railway, or ones belonging to rivals such as the LNWR. Unhappy with this situation, it desired an independent line between the two large settlements, and it opened such a line from Trafford Park to Cressington in March of that year.

At Cressington it met the Liverpool Extension Railway, and at the same time, a line from Glazebrook to Skelton Junction for goods. The junction was east of the site chosen for a station, and was sandwiched between two road bridges. In 1879, west of the station was the departure point of a line to Wigan and St Helens. In some respects, therefore, for decades before World War II, Glazebrook was an interchange point for passengers, but it never achieved the suffix "Junction" for some reason.

Glazebrook West Junction, 1963. Standing in the "V" created by the junction of the line to Wigan with the main line, at about a quarter to one on a Saturday afternoon, we are witnesses to the noon train from Liverpool slowing down ready to stop. The Dam Lane bridge necessitates railway structures having to reach skyward for visibility. The signalman has pulled lever no 40 to allow the main line's home signal to be lowered, and the train will proceed into the station just under the bridge. The Cheshire Lines concrete post lower quadrant signals stand sentry-like, guarding the junction. As the Liverpool suburban stations will have been served by a train some eighteen minutes earlier, this train will omit most of them, but will be all-stations from Hough Green. After Glazebrook, it will turn south-east to continue to Stockport to arrive at 1.25pm. *(E Bentley)*

There are two junctions just west of Glazebrook station creating a triangle of lines.

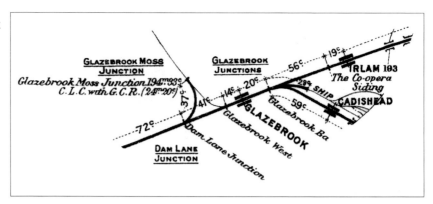

At around a mile from the station is **Dam Lane Junction** *(this page, upper)* with a pair of lines curving north from the main Liverpool to Manchester main line. Opened in 1900 by the Cheshire Lines Railway, this junction was controlled by a brick-based signalbox tall enough to enable the signalmen to see over the adjacent road bridge. Its 25 levers were moved to this 1961 replacement about 150 yards east of the old box (note the BR tubular signal post).
(MA King)

At just a stone's throw from the station is **Glazebrook West Junction** *(this page, lower)* seen in 1959. Its height allows those inside to see the trains they are controlling, and the signals are such that they can be seen by the train crews. Leaving the main line is the 2.15pm from Irlam, heading for Wigan Central with Ivatt 2-6-0 46448 in charge. At the opening, there was a signalbox opposite the station's goods yard, but with the construction of the Wigan branch in 1829, it was moved west for safety reasons, and rebuilt as a three-storey box.
(R Hinton)

A 1956 view of **Glazebrook Moss Junction** *(opposite page, top)* shows where the lines met, 37 chains (almost half a mile) from Dam Lane to the right, with West Junction (also 37 chains) straight on.
(Signalling Record Society, Scrimgeour Collection)

Traversing the Curve, 1955.
(opposite page, bottom)
Fairburn tank 2-6-4T 42235 leaves Glazebrook station and West Junction with a train from Manchester Central to Wigan Central. The line to Liverpool is to the left.
(E Bentley)

Glazebrook, 1949. Just pulling away from the Liverpool platform past the entrance to the small goods yard is a train from Stockport on 26th March. Hauling it is LNER 4-4-0 class D10 62658 *Prince George*, then based at Trafford Park shed. The basic service consisted of four trains, augmented by three more on Saturdays. Stopping at most of the nineteen stations was to take over ninety minutes, and some trains fitted in with stopping services from Warrington. *(Alex Appleton)*

Glazebrook, 1946. Having arrived with the 9.10am train from Wigan Central, the engine prepares to return the service. LNER 0-6-0 5176 has organized the coaches on the down main line, and is starting the process of running round them. They will be pushed back into the station before picking up passengers and departing west. Note the trolley, fully-laden with parcels, and the iron gents urinals on the up platform. On the left, to the rear of the engine, is a siding that led to a small turntable for turning engines such as these. At one time there was a two-road engine shed just under the bridge to the west of the station. *(HC Casserley)*

Glazebrook, around 1912. Looking towards Manchester, this view shows the typical Cheshire Lines buildings and their arrangements. Passengers for Manchester and Stockport have the benefit of just a small shelter whereas the Liverpool-bound customer has the full range of services. A small goods yard was just to the right, accessed by a trailing connection from the main lines. This part of the line to Cressington Junction, Liverpool, opened to passengers on 1st August 1873, five months after goods trains had first used the line. The section east to Cornbrook opened a month later, Glazebrook station opening at the same time. The platform seat has the station name carved in its backrest, and notice how each platform had its access from Glazebrook Lane. *(Lens of Sutton Collection)*

Glazebrook, 1959. Passing west is a trainload of steel running as trip No 81, most probably from Irlam steel works, a short distance to the east. The headlamp code on Stanier 8F 2-8-0 48528 indicates that the brakes of the wagons are connected, so the train is "fitted". A similar train of empty wagons is passing on the up line. Ahead of it is the junction, and just visible through the bridge are the signals for it. The train, with its tender first, has just passed under the signals by the Glazebrook Lane road bridge. Here, splitting distants were used to indicate which route the train was to take. Using three arms instead of the conventional four saved money, equipment and space in the signalbox. *(R Kaye)*

Leaving Glazebrook, 1957. Viewed from Dam Lane bridge is Stanier 2-6-4T 42448 racing through the station heading west. Then, as now, Intercity trains didn't stop here; this is the 1.30pm from Manchester to Liverpool. With stops at Warrington and Widnes (North) the journey took 45 minutes. The limited freight facilities consisted of a small loading dock, a small cattle pen and a long siding on the right. Some cattle wagons and vans occupy it, while a coal wagon is being unloaded. Hidden by the loading gauge is a 5-ton crane. Unlike most railways, the Cheshire Lines wasn't absorbed by one of the Big Four under the Railways Act of 1921. Instead, its management was split between the LMS and the LNER. It was only Nationalization in 1948 that gave sole control of the system to one body – the one based on the former LMS. *(BWL Brooksbank)*

Glazebrook, around early 1940s. Heading west is an express train with Class 5 4-6-0 5023 in charge. Note the cute lattice signal post controlling the small goods yard. The engine is passing over a trailing crossover between the down and up main lines. A reversal would be necessary to access it, controlled by a ground signal – the small white disc on the left. When the signalman in West Junction signalbox pulled lever no 23, the disc would rotate anti-clockwise, and the red stripe would be in the "off" position. *(CM & JM Bentley)*

Glazebrook, c.1960. Looking west from the Glazebrook Lane bridge, this view shows this unassuming station well. The main buildings are on the Liverpool platform, and there is just a small shelter for the Manchester platform, which one might expect to be more patronized. The encouragement to "Park 'n' ride" is receiving little patronage, as the cycle store on the Liverpool platform appears to be empty. Stanier 2-6-2T 40124 arrives with a stopping train for Manchester Central station. Ahead were Irlam & Cadishead, Flixton, Chassenden Road, Urmston and Trafford Park & Stretford stations, with the terminus being 25 to 30 minutes away. Under the next bridge can be seen the start of the pointwork for West Junction. *(BKB Green)*

Glazebrook Station, 1975. Today, the only access to the station is by a small road from Glazebrook Lane, past the small group of white railway cottages on the left. The twin-gabled brick building, with its distinctive bargeboard, stands out proudly. As an unstaffed halt, passengers simply turn up and catch their train at the respective platform; for eastbound travellers, a small shelter suffices. Today, the station is only served by trains every other hour in both directions along the main line. Sparse as this seems, passenger numbers increased by 50% in the

middle of the first decade of the 21st century. The white feature on the wall is a drinking fountain, which still exists, and has the date of construction on it. Other stations had them as well, for example, Padgate and Flixton. *(BPC)*

East of Glazebrook, 1957. This was the view looking from the overbridge at the end of the station on 21st June around ten past three. Stanier 2-6-2T 40097 is pulling the 2.48pm from Manchester Central, and its destination, Warrington Central, will be reached in 15 minutes. Hidden away on the left behind the signals, is the East Junction signalbox. Of 1893 vintage, the 32-lever box will last four more years before it is replaced by a flat-roofed type, similar to the one at Dam Lane featured earlier. *(BWL Brooksbank)*

Signals at Glazebrook East Junction. The company had its own signal depot at Battersby Lane, Warrington. Protecting the junction was this fine set of signals which (unusually) were upper-quadrant. Seen from the rear, the routes are Cadishead and Skelton Junction (left-hand post), Irlam and Manchester (right-hand post) with the smaller arms indicating access to the exchange sidings. *(A Johnson)*

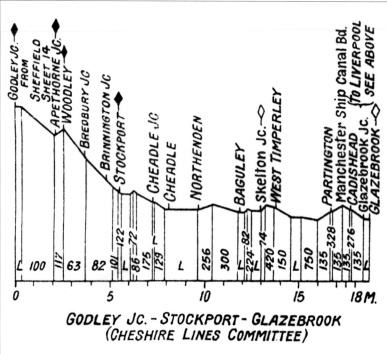

GODLEY JC. - STOCKPORT - GLAZEBROOK
(CHESHIRE LINES COMMITTEE)

Origin and Destination of Traffic West of Glazebrook

Haydock Colliery Wagon. To serve collieries in the Makerfield and West Leigh areas of south Lancashire, the Wigan Junction Railway was promoted in 1873. It was to be double track from the CLR at Glazebrook, but progress was slow (partly due to boggy ground) so it wasn't until 1879 that goods and mineral traffic were carried; the extension from Ince into Wigan took another six years. An Act of 1885 (renewed in 1889) led to a line from St Helens to the Wigan Junction Railway at Lowton St Mary's. Goods and minerals were carried from 1895, and racecourse traffic from 1899, with the whole line formally opening at the very start of 1900. Both lines connected with practically every colliery in the area, and from 1904 the GCR took them over.

St Helens Central, 1956. 40,000 people travelled to the races at Haydock Park when that section of the line was opened in 1899. In later days, after delivering the spectators, trains would pull forward and run round their coaches at Ashton-in-Makerfield or go to St Helens for servicing in steam days. Here, taking on water and coal, is Ivatt 2-4-2T 41289 in late September. While the race meeting was in progress, return trains would assemble west of Ashton-in-Makerfield station, and then when the meeting was over, move forward into Haydock Park station. *(B Hilton)*

Haydock Park, 1960. Passenger services from St Helens stopped in 1952 and from Wigan in 1964, but coal traffic went on for a lot longer. A trainload of steel-bodied coal wagons is brought through the racecourse platforms *en-route* to Golbourne and the LNWR line. West of the station was a platform serving just the down line, probably for unloading horse boxes. The station operated departures effectively as two single lines. There were to be two trains to the east, the 5pm express and the 5.10 stopping train. The last excursion ran in 1963, but in 1975, Ashton station was used for an experiment for race specials on five days – never to be repeated. *(J Peden)*

Goods Provision in Warrington, 1982. Although the line opened in 1873, these imposing structures weren't built until 1897. *(Upper)* Facing the passenger station buildings was this imposing goods office. On the left was the entrance to the goods yard in which was the magnificent goods depot. *(Lower)* Of the two seemingly-cloned warehouses on the line, this was the smaller one at around 200ft by 50ft. Lines entered the middle of the building with unloading docks being accessed through the doors on the sides. Illustrating one of the town's key industries are coils of steel wire in the flat wagons, which would be unloaded by the cranes. Incidentally, a breakdown crane is at the far end of the building. The writing on the walls of both buildings makes interesting reading – the date is after the formation of the GCR, unlike that on Brunswick's wall. While the end panel of the goods shed is plain to see, the four on the sides carried the names of the three owning companies, the far left being the same as the ends. Together with some adjacent land, the warehouse is now a block of flats.
(Both, A Sommerfield)

Brunswick Goods Shed, 1950s. The small building on the left was the original passenger terminus of the St Helens Canal & Railway line, which opened in 1864. Ten years later, the line was extended from near here into central Liverpool, mostly in tunnels, and this station was closed to passengers. Around it was built this magnificent goods shed. Of the two similar warehouses on the line, this was the larger at around 300ft by 550ft. The length enabled the owners to proudly display their presence by writing their names in full, lengthways. The end panels had "Cheshire Lines" written on them.
(R Carpenter)

Halewood Sidings, 1959. At Halewood, a connection, the North Liverpool Extension line linked the main line with the company's warehouses and docks at Huskisson, the MR Sandon Docks, Aintree and Southport. Freight services along the Glazebrook to Godley line could go directly there or be remarshalled at the extensive sidings here. A triangle of lines was created on top of the spoil from Brunswick engine shed, with trains from Liverpool Central passing to Gatacre, Aintree and Southport. It was much quicker to go to the latter by electric train from Exchange station, so this service disappeared in the early 1950s. Here LNER O2 class 2-8-0 63612 hauls a train of tube wagons past the sidings along the down main goods line. *(J Peden)*

Brunswick Sidings, 1957.
Many of the coal trains using the Glazebrook to Godley line would have ended up here, next to the Herculaneum docks. Heading east on the up main line past the sidings on the left, is a trainload of empty wagons hauled by Midland 4F 0-6-0 43847. On the right is Brunswick engine shed, squashed in between the sandstone rocks and the main lines. It consisted of five dead-end roads, a turntable and a coaling stage; the roof looks new, having been constructed only a year previously. Unusually, as it was "built-to-fit" the location, the shed is on a curve – it is far easier to construct sheds on straight lines! *(J Peden)*

Aintree Station, 1959. The racecourse at Aintree had several stations nearby. The L&YR had Sefton Arms station on its main line from Preston, and Racecourse station was accessible from its line from Manchester. The Cheshire Lines station, Central since 1950, was on the line to Southport, and was connected to the main line at Halewood. Looking south from Park Road, this view shows the long platforms needed. In 1933 (see notice) 27 special trains arrived from Manchester (6); London, Marylebone (2) and Kings Cross (the latter with Pullman coaches); Leicester; Leeds; Darlington; Cleethorpes; Bridlington and Scunthorpe. Most travelled over the Godley to Glazebrook section, and four trains ran from Southport along Cheshire Lines. The climax of the Spring Meeting was the Grand National, which was then run on a Friday. *(Hugh Davies)*

Huskisson, 1952. After passing through eastern Liverpool, the line from Halewood turns west and south to end up at a large, 25-acre expanse that opened in 1880. At Foster Street, next to Huskisson, there are lairages capable of accommodating 1,200 cattle, establishing the dock as one of the premier centres for the importation of Irish cattle. There were also many sheds. Although only about 1½ miles from Central station in Liverpool as the crow flies, it was 11 miles by train! Not surprisingly, a passenger service from here was short-lived. *(BPC)*

Sandon Docks, 1960. A short distance north of the lines curving to Huskisson, a branch was built by the Midland Railway to its Sandon Docks. Typical of the engines used there is this ex-L&Y "Pug" 0-4-0ST 51206 pulling a flat wagon with two wooden crates on it. The short wheelbase of these engines enabled them to move about the yard uninhibited by the sharp curves. *(JK Williams)*

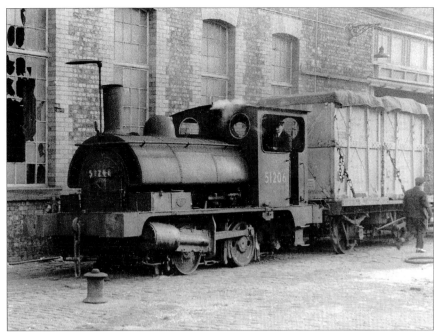

Birkenhead, 1966. The flow of livestock from Ireland to the LNER system via Godley utilized the extensive lairages and slaughterhouses at Wallasey and Woodside. In 1928, the landings there were 249,773 cattle, 47,586 pigs and 368,450 sheep. Slightly more than half were slaughtered, and the rest, after being fed and watered, were dispatched by rail. It was the company's special trains and methods of operation that overcame competition. Movement along other company's lines would be needed to access the Cheshire Lines at Skelton Junction. Leaving Birkenhead is the 7.45pm freight – note the first four wagons, some of which appear to have livestock in them. Standard class 9F 2-10-0 92167 is passing the engine shed. *(Brian Taylor)*

Risley. Just over two miles west of Glazebrook was the site chosen for a Royal Ordnance Factory where bombs were filled. It was approved in 1939, and opened the next year, the rumour being that the site was chosen as it was frequently shrouded in mist, and therefore "invisible" to enemy bombers. Occupying a site in excess of 700 acres, a sum of £13.39M (probably about £650M at today's prices) was spent on construction within six months! At its peak, something like 30,000 people worked there – mostly women doing dangerous work. The depot accessed the main line, and a station was opened on 2nd April 1940, not closing until 1964! There was also a platform on the Glazebrook to Wigan line. The complex had its own internal rail system with up to 14 engines, mostly diesels, but with at least six 0-4-0ST steam engines. All the materials went in and out by rail, as well as many thousands of workers on special trains, some of which arrived and departed along the line to Godley, but as with all wartime events, details are shrouded in secrecy. The current Birchwood station is in the former MoD site. (This picture has been used before, but no other photograph has become available to show the station at Risley.) *(BPC)*

Southport, Two Days before Closure in 1952. Even though the L&YR had a terminus, Chapel Street, in the town, which was well-served by lines to Preston, Liverpool and Manchester, the Cheshire Lines also operated a service to the town. **External View.** Their terminus station on Lord Street was an imposing building with its tall clock tower and frontage onto one of the town's prestigious streets. Opening in 1885, it couldn't compete for services to the two major cities, but it was useful for excursion trains at weekends and in the summer. **Interior View.** Boasting five roads, on one Bank Holiday before the Great War it is estimated that between 40,000 and 50,000 passengers were handled. So busy was the town, and so sure was the new British Railways of attracting custom that the platforms were lengthened in 1949. This was the spacious interior on 5th January, but it closed two days later, becoming a bus depot. *(Both, RK Blencowe)*

City of Liverpool. Granted city status in 1880, Liverpool had been the hub of passenger traffic to Isle of Man, Ireland and across the Atlantic Ocean for decades before. Central station is on the right, and it would be through its doors that many passengers from eastern Europe would have walked having travelled around Manchester on the line from Godley, after their arrival at the east coast ports.

Origin and Destination of Traffic East of Glazebrook

Irlam, 1937. This view is west, towards Glazebrook, from the wooden barrow crossing between the two platforms. We are standing with the base of the 1 in 135 gradient behind us, and with the lines rising to pass over the Manchester Ship Canal "Deviation No 5", to come down to earth just in time to serve Flixton station. Before that "ditch" was constructed, the lines were slightly to the left. The development of the bridge over the canal resulted in the lines being slewed to the right, and a new set of station buildings being constructed. On the left, on the down side, were

sidings, as many services originated or terminated here due to many passengers working in the adjacent steel works. *(Lens of Sutton)*

Irlam Steel Works, 1954. Of all the industries that established themselves on the banks of the canal, arguably Partington Iron & Steel works had the most profound effect on the rail network. The other major player was Partington coal basin. On the right are the blast furnaces with the mills (the large shed in the centre behind the water and cooling towers). In 1913, Pearson & Knowles Coal & Iron Co Ltd built a steel works occupying over 100 acres, and bounded by the two main railway lines, the A57 and the ship canal. Originally, it was serviced by the Cheshire Lines and the Ship Canal Railway. Many of the raw materials, coal, limestone and scrap iron, were transported by rail along all or part of the Glazebrook to Godley line. In May 1930, the Lancashire Steel Corporation Ltd was formed by the amalgamation of the Partington Iron & Steel Co with Pearson & Knowles and the Wigan Coal & Iron Co. By 1935, the new works was one of the most modern and integrated iron and steel works in the country. During the dock strike in 1967, the MSC outlet could not be used, so 1,291 railway wagons conveyed the steel to

Immingham Docks. At its peak, in 1967, 670,000 tons of steel were produced, the industry being nationalized that year. Much of the finished output (half a million tons) was taken to Warrington for finishing. During the late 1960s, the industry went into serious decline, and although the Irlam Works was profitable it didn't figure in any future plans. Many men were made redundant in 1972 and 1974, and the plant finally closed in 1979. Roads in Irlam have names like Bessemer Road and Darby Road, reflecting processes that were employed. *(B Roberts)*

Moving the Goods, 1955. Internal movements in the plant were done by a handful of ageing steam locos, two of which are featured here. In the places with the sharpest curves, two 0-4-0STs would be used to shunt the "tappings" of the blast furnace to the steel works in ladles – careful shunting was absolutely necessary! Engine No 14 was built by Hudswell Clarke with No 6 being a Peckett engine. Where more power was needed, for example, to move raw materials or finished products, a more powerful engine like No 13 (another Peckett engine) was used. On its tanks are the initials for the Lancashire Steel Corporation, but in some places, marks are discernable from the previous owner, Partington Iron & Steel Co. Diesels took over from 1953. *(Both, BPC)*

Manchester Ship Canal Railways, Irlam, 1957. Whilst the steel works engines tended to not to stray too far, engines belonging to the Ship Canal company were often seen on other railway companies' lines – note the cooling and water towers in the background. This is one of 22 Hudswell-Clarke engines called "Long Tanks" to differentiate them from their predecessors, which could only carry 260 gallons less, their side tanks only extending to between the front and middle wheels. Originally called *St Petersburg*, it was numbered 62 when the MSC fleet of engines were given numbers in 1914/5. *(J Peden)*

Co-operative Wholesale Society, Irlam Soap Works. Many industries were established along the banks of the canal and around the two truncated parts of the original line – one such industry was British Tar Products at Cadishead. Much of their raw materials and products passed along the railways. They had a fleet of 136 tank wagons in 1936, and prior to the outbreak of World War II, carried 38,440 tons of tar. They also made creosote and distilled benzol, both of which could be termed "bad neighbour" industries. The CWS established a soap and candle factory next to the redundant original line west of the bridge, and later, a margarine works. Both factories had internal rail systems, the Ship Canal company granting running powers over the branches from Irlam. The original lines around the site of the old station served as exchange sidings between the Ship Canal

and Cheshire Lines. A set of wooden steps was built to enable a special train to ferry workers (manual and office) from the station to the soap works. This fine 6-wheel coach was built by the MR at Derby in 1885; the engine is one of two Peckett 0-4-0STs dating from 1951. In 1900, 700 people worked in the soap works, rising to 1,200 by 1950. Due to road competition the CWS's internal rail system contracted, the last "Soap Works Special" running in 1959, and the whole system closing in 1965. After withdrawal in 1960, the coach was restored, and is now part of the NRM collection. The engine went to the Dunlop Rubber Co in 1967. *(BPC)*

Along the Cheshire Lines Railway from Glazebrook towards Godley

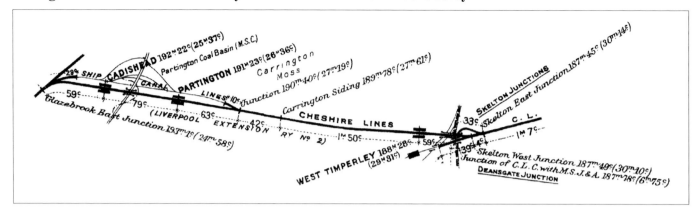

Cadishead, 1977. This view shows the line as built in 1873 and subsequent additions. Looking east, we see the deviation in all its glory. Straight ahead are the original lines and the later loops, added to allow the line to serve the industries. On the right, at a higher level, are the elevated lines leading up to the bridge. *(D Thorpe)*

Cadishead, First Station. A passenger-only station opened here with the opening of the line in 1873. The lamps, complete with the station name on them, and the ornate iron work to support the extensive canopies, show up well. After only six years this station closed, to be superseded in 1893 by the second station, 50 yards north, and on an embankment. In contrast to the first station, the second one had only small sheds on each platform, similar to those at Partington. *(BPC)*

Cadishead, 1958. The time is approximately 12.23pm, and arriving at Cadishead is the 12.20pm SO from Glazebrook to Stockport. Stanier 2-6-2T 40094 would take another 30 minutes to complete the journey stopping at Partington, West Timperley, Baguley, Northenden and Cheadle. The basic passenger facilities had oil lamps up to the end on 30th November 1964. The bridge carrying the Liverpool to Manchester main line over the "Ditch" is in the background, and in front of the train is "Deviation No 4". When the Ship Canal was planned, the solution to the 75ft clearance needed for boats was to deviate and elevate the line. A new line from Glazebrook East Junction carried the line at 1 in 135, up and over the canal, coming back down to earth at Partington Junction – a deviation of fractionally over 2½ miles. The new line opened on 27th February 1893, and the new station for passengers on 29th May of the same year. With the original line not closing until after the new line was operational, there was a period of time when both lines were open. *(HC Casserley)*

Cadishead, 1958. Looking east we see the "minimal" passenger facilities provided – on the pre-stressed concrete platforms were two small shelters. Illumination was by gas, and in the distance can be seen the steelwork for the bridge over the canal. A survey conducted the following year found that the station was used by 60 people a week. With 11 trains stopping here each day, that works out at an average of just 1 person per train. *(HC Casserley)*

Cadishead, 1960. An up coal train looks to be emerging from the up through siding and onto the main line through the station. The BR-replacement signals were controlled from the 17-lever signalbox with its standard vertical cladding. The smaller arm indicates a route from the down line into the down through siding. Unless empty wagons could be made into longer trains, the returning empties took up as much space and as many engines as the loaded trains. Heading east is Standard class 2-10-0 92048 on 14th May. Its home shed, 17C, was Rowsley, so the train will probably be leaving the line to Godley at Heaton Mersey East junction, and will then pass through Cheadle Heath and along the MR main line. *(WA Brown)*

Cadishead, 1957. Struggling up the last part of the rising gradient of 1 in 135 is ageing MR 0-6-0 class 4F 43843 hauling a fitted freight. The footplate crew will be glad that the brakes of the wagons can be controlled by the engine when the train starts to descend after crossing the bridge over the canal. The distant signal is interesting –the steel tubular post has been painted to make sure the signal is seen. With the sky is behind it, a solitary arm in the air could easily be overlooked. *(J Peden)*

Deviation Bridge No 4, 1958. The steelwork for the high-level bridges was done by the Glasgow firm of Sir William Arrol & Co. This bridge has brick arches on either side, giving a pleasing symmetrical appearance. The bridges were built wide enough to carry four tracks, even though only two were ever laid, indicating the thoughts of the railway companies for future business. The lines we are travelling on belong to the Ship Canal company, and Cadishead is to the left with Partington to the right. During the construction of the canal, over 50 million cubic yards of soil and rock were excavated. Some was used to create embankments like this one, with a large amount being used in the Eastham and Runcorn areas to create a barrier to separate the river and the canal. To test the safety of the bridge, ten locomotives of the MS&LR with a total weight of 750 tons, were driven onto it. The canal opened on 1st January 1894, but the official Royal opening was at the convenience of Queen Victoria and the weather. On 21st May she went for a short trip along the canal in the paddle steamer *Enchantress*, and received a 21-gun salute. *(HC Casserley)*

Partington, First Station, 1890. On the other side of the "Ditch" to Cadishead was Partington. The line was moved a short distance north, and elevated to get over the canal. The original and the deviation lines were open for a few months in 1893 because of the resistance of the railway companies to the canal. Having lost the battle in Parliament, they continued their war of attrition wherever they could.

So, when the deviation lines had been built and tested, the Ship Canal (not unnaturally) wanted to shift all the railway traffic onto the new bridges so that they could dig up the old lines that were preventing the completion of the canal on either side. However, the railway companies wanted their "pound of flesh", and refused to use them for anything other than goods for ten weeks. The LNWR was the most hostile to the MSC, and originally wanted a six-month trial period for Deviations 1, 2 and 3, but settled for four months after pressure from the canal company. The external view of the station illustrates the similar appearance to other buildings on the Cheshire Lines Railway. *(Greater Manchester County Record Office)*

Partington, 1952. Looking towards Stockport, this view shows the basic facilities a mile east across the river from Cadishead. A little way east, the original and deviation lines met at Partington Junction. *(HC Casserley)*

Partington, around 1960. Standing at the end of the up platform, the photographer witnesses a train from the Glazebrook direction passing over Manchester Road, and about to enter the station. The signalman in the box at the other end of the station has pulled lever no 2 to raise the signal arm to allow the driver of an unidentified Jubilee 4-6-0 to proceed. The rear of the train has just crossed the Ship Canal with parts of the bridge visible. Down at road level is the cute arch over the entrance to the platform and a notice board, no doubt extolling the virtues of places such as Southport and Liverpool. While the steel works makes up the background, the original line, expanded by numerous sidings, occupies the land in the middle. A white plume of steam betrays the presence of en engine shunting there, perhaps on its way to have a break amongst the buildings at the bottom right. *(N Jones/G Fox Collection)*

Partington Coal Basin, 1929. After passing under Deviation No 4, the canal widened to 250ft for ¾ mile to provide an area where boats could tie up and be loaded with coal (Partington Coal Basin) and to provide space for two ships to pass in the middle. Partington became the nearest port to the Lancashire coalfield, and brought South Yorkshire collieries (for example, Barnsley) 30 miles closer to the sea. At its peak in 1907, exports amounted to just under 1½ million tons. It was after the 1926 coal miners strike that imports reached their peak at 1.2 million tons. With trains carrying over 500 tons of coal, around ten trains a day would arrive here during the peak period. The aerial views on this page and the next give a good idea of the size of the undertaking and the scale of the railway's involvement. *(Copyright Manchester Ship Canal Photographic Archive held at and reproduced courtesy of Greater Manchester County Record Office)*

Operations at Partington Coal Basin. Wagons were shunted onto sidings that funnelled onto one of the tips. There, a man using a rope and capstan, pulled the next wagon onto a turntable, and made sure that the end door was facing the proper direction. After securing the wagon, it was tipped up using a hydraulic hoist, so that the coal went into the hold of the waiting ship – note the lever to operate the capstan by his right foot. The "all-weather" construction of the working area leaves a lot to be desired. *(Don Thorpe)*

Partington Coal Basin, 1950. Originally, there were four tips for loading ships' bunkers with coal (two on each side of the canal) and a steam crane. Two more tips were added in 1907 together with more sidings, which by 1924 had reached a total of almost 25 miles. Both sides of the canal were fed from the Cheshire Lines, either from the north-east at Glazebrook, or from the south at Partington Junction. In 1980 the National Coal Board awarded the contract for exporting coal to Garston, and after a temporary reprieve due to delays completing the works there, the coal basin closed completely on 3rd July 1981. *(Copyright Manchester Ship Canal Photographic Archive held at and reproduced courtesy of Greater Manchester County Record Office)*

Operations at Partington Coal Basin, c.1920. The facilities on the north side were numbered 1, 3 and 5, the two even-numbered tips being to the south. They were operated by hydraulic machinery from Armstrong, Mitchell & Co, forerunners of Armstrong-Whitworth, in 1897. Tips 6 and 7 were added later. The technique of mechanical handling, initially of coal, later applied to other loads, made Manchester a capital intensive port, while Liverpool was labour intensive. Elsecar colliery is near Barnsley.
(Greater Manchester County Record Office)

Loading at Partington Basin. Not just coal was loaded here. These wagons contain soda ash from ICI plants at Northwich – note the covers to protect the load from the elements and to minimize dust. The ship is the Norwegian *Roy*. This close-up of tip no 7 shows a wagon just after being righted, having emptied its load into the hold of the ship. Next, it would slowly trundle down to the sidings to be removed. On the aerial views the rows of sidings feeding the tips and the single run-off siding can clearly be seen. *(Brunner-Mond)*

Partington South Side, 1949. This view is from the main lines after they have passed over the canal and are returning to the original level. Manchester Ship Canal engine No 19 is seen taking a train down to the tips on 26th March. Coal for these tips was easily accessed from the lines from Yorkshire. While the export trade of the canal was dominated (in terms of volume) by bulk loads like coal, the real money exports were cotton and machinery. The ships themselves needed coaling as well, adding to the total amount needed. Just after World War II, the canal company owned over 2,000 wagons for use on its extensive system of lines. *(Alex Appleton)*

Partington Junction, 1976. This was the joining of the original line to the deviation. The lines run down to the south side of Partington Coal Basin and the coal-fired power station. The 24-lever box was closed, prematurely, in 1984 after being set on fire (not an uncommon fate of lightly-used boxes). At its demise, the building had a brick base, which was odd for a Cheshire Lines box. *(ND Mundy)*

Partington Junction, 1965. Steaming east along the up main line is ageing class 5 4-6-0 45139; the point rodding is to the Junction box, on the other side of the line. The signalman at Partington signalbox will have pulled lever no 4 to raise the top signal (with its back to us) and the signalman here, being just ¾ mile away, will have pulled his lever no 21 to raise the lower arm. On the left are a few sidings, while the more extensive lines are to the north side – note the rarely-modelled lights indicating that 24-hour operations were practiced. Sheeting of wagons was done when loads could be affected by the weather. *(CM & JM Bentley)*

Partington Junction, 1965. Awaiting a road is Stanier 8F 2-8-0 48368 on 19th May. On the right is a brick shunters' cabin where food and comfort breaks could be taken, and the engine has pulled up fractionally beyond the water tank. That, and the fully-laden tender, indicates that this engine has probably just come on duty, probably from Heaton Mersey shed. The industrial nature of the area is indicated by the smoking chimneys and structures in the background. Judging by the signals, an up train is expected. On the left are three sidings, accessed from the down main line by the point in front of us with a trailing connection to the up main as well. *(CM & JM Bentley)*

Partington Sidings, 1966. Waiting to depart with one of the endless empty mineral trains is Stanier 8F 2-8-0 48171. Next to where the River Mersey was widened, deepened and straightened to form part of the Ship Canal was the site chosen to build a coal-fired power station. Conceived as an alternative for Barton power station, it was developed by Manchester Corporation in 1916. Little was done until after World War II when the British Electric Authority opened "A" station with a capacity of 240MW in 1956. Its identical sister was never built, and the site closed in 1991. However, a 860MW station is to be built on the site, but it will be gas-fired. *(CM & JM Bentley)*

Narrow Gauge Railway across Carrington Moss. Towards the end of the last century, the rapidly expanding City of Manchester was fast running out of places to get rid of its refuse, particularly its "night soil". The City bought 1,100 acres of Carrington Moss in 1885, and it absorbed much clinker in the construction of roads and a 6-mile, 2ft 6in gauge, rail network across the Moss. Barges were loaded at the Water Street depot in central Manchester, and unloaded at Carrington Wharf on the Ship Canal. Material was also sent by rail, being loaded at Ardwick, and then transferred to the moss railway at Carrington Exchange Sidings. The system was worked by 0-4-0STs with a wagon for extra water and coal. They would pull 15 to 20 4-wheel open wagons to the tipping area, and after leaving them there, go back to the wharf sidings and collect some more. This view is of the 1888 WG Bagnall engine *Robinson*, the second one on the network, and renamed from another of the Cleaning Committee's Councillors, *Grantham*. The last loads were tipped in 1937, and the land reverted to first-class agricultural status. The exchange sidings were used for many years for wagon storage. *(Manchester Cleansing Department)*

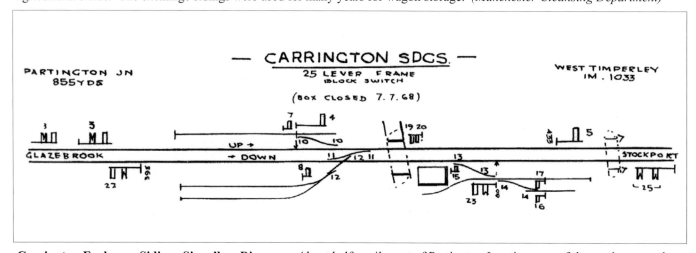

Carrington Exchange Sidings Signalbox Diagram. About half a mile east of Partington Junction, one of the roads across the Moss crosses the line. At the level crossing, sidings were built, controlled by this 25-lever box. *(Signalling Record Society)*

West Timperley, 1961.
Looking west towards Glazebrook we see class 5 4-6-0 44715 with a load of hoppers on their way towards Skelton Junction. Opening with the commencement of passenger services along the line, the size of the wooden buildings shows that more passengers were expected than at any of the stations to the west. Three-quarters of a mile east the line met the original Stockport, Timperley & Altrincham Railway at Skelton East Junction. The Liverpool platform has a replacement shelter with the 12-lever signalbox at

the end – tall Cheshire Lines signals still rule though. There were no goods facilities at the station. In 1960, residents of the area were fortunate to be served by a Saturdays-only service from Leicester to Blackpool (9.38am) with the return at 11.57am, hopefully after a relaxing week at the seaside. Alternatively, a summer day-trip to Southport would entail departure at 11.07am, returning at 8.58pm. Nearby was the rail-served Carrington Power station. This had a short life, being built in the 1950s and accessed from Partington Junction, as was the chemical plant developed on nearby land. It was mothballed in the 1980s after being used for fuel experiments; demolition followed. After closure to passenger trains on 30th November 1964, the line carried a lot of traffic, mainly to Irlam steelworks and Carrington power station. When the steelworks closed in the early 1970s, the line was cut back to a single track to serve the Shell plant at Carrington with trainloads of propylene arriving from South Wales. Even that has ceased, but there is talk of the Rover Group taking over the former power station site as a distribution depot. Maybe, trains will run again over this section. *(Stations UK)*

West Timperley, 1947. The line was built on an embankment here, as it will soon cross over the Bridgewater canal and two sets of railway lines. The second is the MSJ&AR, the first being a short loop from Timperley Junction on the MSJ&AR, up to Broadheath Junction on the LNWR line to Warrington. At the end of the platforms, the line passes over the Manchester Road

as seen in this view south-east. For some time after opening, the station was known as "West Timperley for Bowden". Quite why the signals facing us are so tall is a mystery, as there appear to be no sighting problems. While the top arm would have been operated by the signalbox here, the lower distant arm is operated by the signalman in the box in front (Skelton Junction). Note the name of the station carved into the benches. The area is renowned for its "Timperley Early" rhubarb. *(Stations UK)*

West Timperley Line, 1966. "Austerity" 2-8-0 90113 is signalled to take the Cheshire Lines route west with a load of power station coal for Carrington on 12th March. This engine entered service as 7015 in March 1943 from the North British Locomotive Co, and while many of the same batch saw service abroad, 7015 went to the Longmoor Military Railway for instructional purposes. After the war, it was loaned by the War Department to the GWR for a year, and ended its days shedded at Wakefield before being withdrawn in September 1966. When devised by

the Ministry of Supply, they were to be made to minimal standards and poorer quality materials, hence the name. The basic idea was for an engine capable of hauling loads of 1,000 tons at 40mph; many of the parts were to be prefabricated and assembled with the minimum of labour. The thought in the planners' minds was that after the war abroad, these engines were expendable just like tanks and guns. The designer, Riddles, made the chimney small and squat – critics were expecting an engine similar to the Southern Railway Q1 class, but they were to be disappointed! *(N Spilsbury)*

Skelton Junction, 1905. This magnificent view is from the signalbox next to Moss Lane bridge looking west towards Glazebrook. Off to the left is the 1866 link to the LNWR line at Broadheath, and the middle set of lines are part of the 1873 line to Glazebrook. On the right is the oldest line, the 1865 Stockport, Timperley & Altrincham Railway, curving away to pass under the other two lines to Deansgate Junction, where it would join the 1849 MSJ&AR. Recently closed at the time of the photograph would be the curve from the latter line, from approximately the right hand end of the wooden footbridge north to Timperley, in the background. Notice the two distinct types of signal. On the left, dating from 1866 are the taller lattice posts with lower repeater arms (they are on the wrong side of the track to aid sighting) whereas the original line, to the right, has shorter posts. All of the arms would be lower quadrant. The wooden footbridge carries a pathway connecting Brookfield Road, on the right, over the original lines, and then under the later additions by a subway to Bridge Grove on the left. Just south of the line was Pickering Lodge, the home of an important landowner, John Skelton, whose name was used to identify the junction. *(J Ryan collection)*

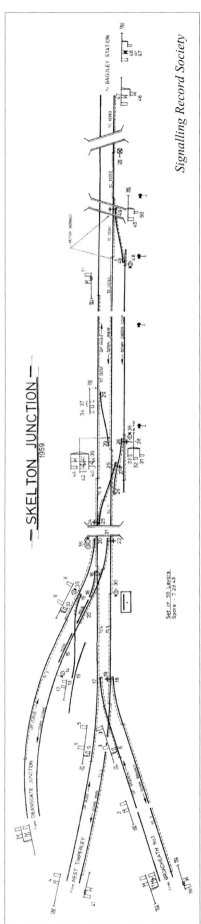

Signalling Record Society

Skelton Junction, 1976. What a wonderful building this was. Lines from the MSJ&AR at Deansgate Junction and the LNWR from Broadheath met here to create Skelton Junction, and hence the signalbox was needed. Further lines to Glazebrook (1873) and Timperley (1878) increased the number of levers in the box to 50. Its vertical wooden boarding would have been painted white, while the nameboard was black with white letters. *(ND Mundy)*

Skelton Junction, Interior. Facing out onto the junctions, the signalman had this diagram of the line in front of him above the window. The shelf had instruments to allow communication with the four adjacent signal boxes by ringing bells – each box's name being on a brass plate in front of each instrument. As can be seen, the second lever (no 29) operated the two points for a trailing crossover enabling trains from the sidings in between the running lines to be pushed onto the up main before to restarting in the down direction. Each lever had to be pulled in sequence, and in the locking room beneath the signalbox, there were mechanisms that prevented conflicting train movements to be set up. The glare of the sun setting in the west must have restricted visibility, and the newspaper would possibly help keep the box cooler in the summer as well! In addition to pulling the levers and recording each train in a register, the signalman would be required to observe the tail light on each train to ensure it hadn't become divided. *(GH Platt, Eddie Johnson Collection)*

Connections to the Manchester South Junction & Altrincham Railway

With the connection between the Liverpool & Manchester Railway and the Leeds & Manchester Railway opening in 1844, cross-Pennine travel became possible. This left the two companies that shared London Road station, isolated and unable to access the port of Liverpool. They agreed to build a line from London Road to meet the Liverpool & Manchester line at Ordsall Lane – the "South Junction" part. However, they also built a branch from Castlefield Junction, almost paralleling the Bridgewater Canal to the small market town of Altrincham; this opened on 20th July 1849. The Glazebrook to Godley line passed over it, and a link came down from Skelton Junction to meet it at Deansgate Junction.

Timperley, 1931. This sight is about to be consigned to history. Stanier 2-6-2Ts were regular hauliers of the service on this intensive suburban service on a line built as an afterthought between Manchester London Road station and Altrincham. Electrification in 1931 did not remove steam-hauled services along the line – at its southern end it continued to Chester. A regular service between Manchester Central station and Chester developed, often the trains running limited- or non-stop until Altrincham, and then all-stations to Chester. Motive power, from Trafford Park shed, was often an ex-LNER D class 4-4-0 engine. *(ER Morten)*

Deansgate Junction, 1956. Approximately 200 yards south of Timperley Junction, a curve swings in from the east; this is the line from Stockport. Opening in 1865, the Stockport, Timperley & Altrincham Railway joined the MSJ&AR at Deansgate Junction. Between the two junctions are two overbridges. Just visible on the right is the bridge carrying the link from Skelton Junction, west to Broadheath and Warrington, while beyond it (out of sight) is the Cheshire Lines route from Skelton Junction to Glazebrook. Looking north in February we see the original signalbox and the gate keeper's cottage, where Deansgate Lane crosses the line. The following year, the box was resited on the opposite side of the lines.
(Signalling Record Society, Scrimgeour Collection)

Timperley Junction, 1952. In the background are two bridges on Park Road. On the left is the older one, crossing the Bridgewater canal, and on the right, a bridge dating from 1849 passes over the MSJ&AR. Timperley station is just beyond this right-hand bridge. Between us and the bridges is a signalbox with lines on either side. On the right is the line to Altrincham, while on the left is the chord that passes under the Cheshire Lines route from Glazebrook. At Broadheath, it will meet the line from Skelton Junction that continues west as the LNWR to Warrington. These fine signals protect the up line at the junction – the tall arm is the home signal and the lower is a repeater to help sighting. *(R Gee)*

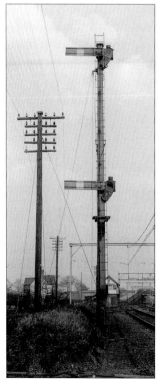

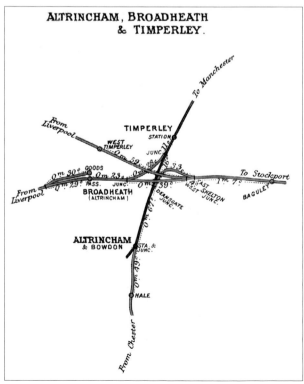

ALTRINCHAM, BROADHEATH & TIMPERLEY.

Altrincham Gas Works Engine, 1947. In 1847, a field on Moss Lane was built on to provide gas for Altrincham and district. The growth of the company can be seen by the amount of gas produced:

1872   17 million cu ft
1880   28 million cu ft
1900   145 million cu ft
1920   262 million cu ft
1933   457 million cu ft

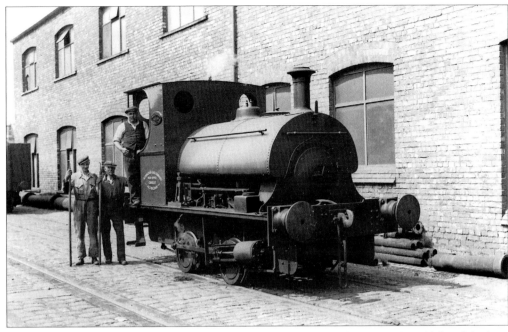

Much of the coal would arrive in trains passing from the Godley direction, and then swinging south at Skelton Junction. Due to the rising demand for its product, and the problems and expense of unloading coal from wagons at the goods yard by the station, the company built a single standard-gauge line down the middle of the lane in 1893. Horses were the motive power for over thirty years until a Sentinel steam lorry was introduced. This was superseded twenty years later by this Peckett 0-4-0ST named *Arthur E. Potts* after one of the company's directors. It would make a handful of trips from the sidings to the gas works each day, but it tended to derail easily when it met the tramway lines. Eventually, the engine was sold to Preston Docks, being replaced by a Sentinel steam engine. The works closed in 1958. *(Alex Appleton)*

Altrincham, 1930. Looking north from Moss Lane, this view shows the situation prior to electrification. On the left is the main departure platform for Manchester – hence its length and large canopy. Down trains arrived at the left-hand side of the island platform in the middle of the picture. The lines continue south from the station controlled by South box at the end of the platform on the right. Those on the left went to a carriage shed on the site of the original station a short distance away. It is the pair in the middle of the picture that interest us most. They continue to Northwich and Chester, being part of the Cheshire Midland Railway and West Cheshire Railways before they became part of the Cheshire Lines Railway in 1865. Passenger trains from Piccadilly now connect with the Godley to Glazebrook line at Northenden Junction, and exit at Skelton Junction to ferry passengers to Chester. *(Stations UK)*

Northwich, 1955. After leaving Altrincham, hoppers of coal climb Hale bank, and continue their journey south-west to Northwich in the salt mining area of Cheshire. Heading west, about to pass through the station, is Robinson class O4 7F 2-8-0 63794 on a hot summer day on 20th August. The headlamps indicate that at least a third of the wagons' brakes are connected to that of the engine, enabling higher speeds to be run. Central Cabin is on the right. *(Brian Morrison)*

Northwich, 1948. Sometimes hopper wagons were left in loops to the east of the station and tripped to Winnington works by other engines – the same happened with empty wagons as seen here. The driver of Robinson L3 2-6-4T class 9062 is having a discussion with the shunting staff, probably about where to put his nine hoppers. The sidings at Oakleigh could handle 14 wagons, so when (as was normal) 24 arrived on a train, they had to be split. This and a sister engine arrived in 1943 to bank trains up the 1 in 53 gradient. When a trainload had been assembled in the loops, an engine would be attached, and it would trundle back through Altrincham to regain the Glazebrook to Godley line at Skelton Junction. *(RJ Buckley, Initial Photographics)*

End of the Journey, 1960. This activity is still being enacted. While the motive power, wagons and clothes of the staff may all have changed, the arrival of a train load of crushed limestone from the Peak District still continues, to the tune of five million tons annually. Here, at Winnington, to the west of Northwich, a trainload of special hopper wagons has arrived on 9th July. A very clean Stanier 8F 2-8-0 48340 has brought its train into one of the four loops to the north of the main line via Hartford & Greenbank East Junction on the ex-Cheshire Midland line from Altrincham to Chester. *(WA Brown)*

The "Circular Service" Using Junctions at Timperley & Skelton

In 1879, the MS&LR squashed in another junction curve between Timperley station and Timperley Junction. Known as the MSJ&AR or Timperley Curve, it was used from 1st December by a Manchester circular service. This went from London Road to Woodley, thence to Stockport Tiviot Dale to Manchester Central. However, it was not well patronized, so on 20th March the following year the service was withdrawn. In 1903, the junction at Timperley was closed and removed soon afterwards, while the section from Skelton Junction north was retained as sidings. However, this too was removed by around 1910.

Timperley, 1911. This 6-inch to the mile map illustrates the transport infrastructure wonderfully. First to arrive on the scene was the Bridgewater canal. Having started in the Castlefield area of Manchester it would eventually join the River Mersey at Runcorn. Passenger-carrying boats used to ply the canal, but the journey from end to end would take most of a working day. Paralleling the canal is the railway line from Manchester to Altrincham, dating from 1849, and passing from top to bottom on the map. Next in the area was a line from the east, the Stockport, Timperley & Altrincham Railway, which opened in 1865; it joined the

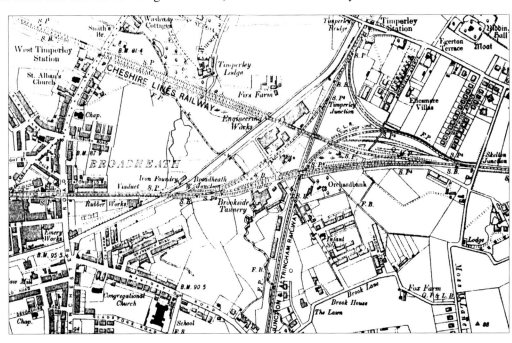

MSJ&AR at Deansgate Junction. North of it was Timperley station and south of it was Timperley Junction, which was made the next year when the LNWR built its line west to Warrington. It also created Skelton Junction in the same year by opening the short link from Broadheath on the Warrington line to meet the line from the east. In 1873, Skelton Junction became the starting point for the Cheshire Lines connection for the line to Glazebrook. Last to be built, and the first to close, was a short curve from south of Timperley station up to Skelton Junction. *(Reproduced by kind permission of the Ordnance Survey)*

Skelton Junction, 1939. After running fresh from an overhaul at Gorton works, the engine is turned in readiness for the return trip – the fireman is just visible on the left releasing the brake. The locomotive is seemingly a little too heavy for the turntable judging by the apparent (and rather alarming) dip in the middle. Looking at ex-GCR class B1 (later B18) 5195, one can almost sense the pride that many workers had in their job before World War 2. Despite depictions in contemporary postcards, the Cheshire Lines owned no locomotives of its own other than a few Sentinel steam railcars. When the electric units were built for

the main Manchester to Altrincham line, half were to have the driving units at the "Manchester" end, with the rest facing the other way. Sometimes, when units had been refurbished at Horwich, they came back the wrong way round, so were hauled here. Unfortunately, they were too long for the turntable, but all was not lost as the bogies were removed at Altrincham depot and temporary ones put underneath. The unit was then turned here, rebuilt and sent off on its way. *(Kidderminster Railway Museum)*

Connections to the Warrington & Altrincham Railway

From 1854, there had been a line from Timperley, north of Altrincham, through Broadheath and west across the flat Mersey plain to Warrington. In 1866, the Cheshire Lines put in a short connection from Skelton Junction, in the east, to Broadheath so enabling trains to pass from Stockport to Warrington.

Skelton Junction, 1963. Following the withdrawal of passenger train services on 8th September 1962, the line had a healthy level of freight traffic over the next 20 years. Stanier 8F 2-8-0 48338 is well up the stiff 1 in 72 gradient necessary for the line to pass over the Manchester to Altrincham electrified line. The cost of repairing the bridges across "the Ditch" was cited as the main reason for closing the route in 1985. However, it wasn't until June 1997 that dismantling of the high-level bridge at Latchford began. *(P Hutchinson)*

West Timperley line, 1952. For every loaded westbound train, there was an eastbound train of empties. Here, the driver of LMS 0-8-0 49343 has released the brakes of the train, and allows gravity to gently pull the train forwards across the junction. Signals on both this and the line from Timperley were on tall lattice posts with lower repeater arms, the road bridge ahead providing an obstruction to sighting. All three routes from the west had the option of going into the down loop beyond the junction, hence the smaller arm on the bracket. Note the rarely-modelled practice of providing additional support for signal posts in the form of an outrigger with guy wires. *(N Spilsbury)*

Broadheath line. With the time just after 1.45pm, class 5 4-6-0 45350 reduces speed as it descends the gradient that enabled the line to go over the top of the MSJ&AR; ahead is Skelton (East) Junction. Skirting past the rooftops of Timperley, is the SO Llandudno to Sheffield 1E21 on 18th June. Having left the seaside terminus at 11.30, the train would have picked up other holiday makers all the way to Prestatyn. After a stop at Broadheath, its destination would be reached at 3.35pm. The usefulness of the line to Summer Saturday passenger traffic is illustrated by the fact that ten minutes later, the 11.40am from Colwyn Bay would pass by. *(N Spilsbury)*

While the line continues west to Warrington, only a brief snapshot of the railway infrastructure is included until the line arrives at Arpley.

Broadheath Junction, 1961. Broadheath No 1 signalbox stands sentinel-like about ¼ mile before the eastern end of the platforms at the station. Curving away down on the left is the original line from Timperley Junction and the MSJ&AR to Manchester Central. On the right, rising up, and also curving to the left is the 1866 link, built by the Cheshire Lines to Skelton Junction. *(Stations UK)*

Broadheath, 1961. The view is looking west after the line has crossed the Duke of Bridgewater's canal. The line could have opened between here and the Latchford area of Warrington six months before it did, but the lack of completed bridges here, and over the Mersey, meant that it was a railway in the middle of nowhere for that short time. *(Brunel University, Mowat Collection)*

Broadheath, around 1955. Oh for such a facility now in congested South Lancashire! A stopping train, hauled by Ivatt 2-6-2T 41288, pauses at the up platform on its way to Manchester from Warrington. Note the pride in a clean and tidy station with flower beds, seats and water buckets, all still lit by gas. Due to the line being on an embankment, the platforms (made of wood in places) are supported on short brick piles. In the foreground, a wooden crossing made of sleepers is seen in detail. The tall bracket signals behind us are casting a shadow onto the end of the buildings on the left. While the line to Skelton Junction continues straight ahead over the MSJ&AR, this train will turn north, and descend to Timperley Junction on the joint line to Manchester. *(BPC)*

Broadheath, 1964. Residents of Broadheath living slightly west of the station were woken by a loud bang on the evening of 18th January. Jubilee class 4-6-0 45695 *Minotaur*, whilst hauling the 10.40pm Liverpool to York mail train, ran into the back of a goods train that was heading the same way. The goods had arrived at Broadheath No 3 box, and the signalman, who was a relief man, signalled it to stop at the box as he wanted to temporarily cross it over to the down line to accept and pass the mail. He thought that one lever worked both the facing and trailing ends of the crossover, but it did not, and he

only pulled over the trailing end. When he gave a hand signal to the train crew to set back, they actually set back on the line they were on instead of crossing over. Without the benefit of track circuiting, he allowed the mail train to proceed, which hit the goods train in the rear at about 40mph. Cranes from Gorton and Edge Hill arrived, and with the rest of the debris cleared away, the engine was placed into a siding to await its fate – it was decided to scrap it rather than rebuild it.
(G Coltas Collection)

Arpley Junction, 1965. With its rear wagons passing the site of Warrington Arpley station, a loaded coal train heads west. Looking east from the wonderfully-named Slutcher's Lane bridge, we see Standard class 9F 2-10-0 92156 bringing a train that has arrived here by passing along the Glazebrook to Godley line as far as Skelton Junction, then along the LNWR line via Broadheath, Thelwell and Latchford to arrive here. Ahead are the empty platforms at Warrington Bank Quay (Low Level, nos 5 and 6) from where the train could proceed to Fiddlers Ferry power station or Garston's docks. *(JA Oldfield)*

Arpley Sidings, 1966. Meanwhile, looking in the other direction from the bridge we see a train of empty wagons coming out of Arpley sidings, and about to join the line to Skelton Junction just on the other side of the bridge. Standard class 9F 2-10-0 92021 has an odd front end, as it was once modified to test a Crosti boiler. The parachute water tank is well positioned to allow engines to refill their tanks from the chord or the loop on the right. In the background are the sidings that make up some of the sorting sidings for trains still in use today in one of the rail systems busiest marshalling yards. *(WA Brown)*

Walton Junction, 1964. Passenger trains conveying excursions or scheduled trains to the North Wales coast regularly used this route to avoid areas they would only add congestion too. This one, returning to a Yorkshire city, will pass through Arpley Junction and proceed to Skelton Junction to gain the Glazebrook to Godley line. It would have arrived here along the Birkenhead Joint line from Chester, going along "Deviation No 2" to pass Acton Grange Junction, and then over the Manchester Ship canal. At Walton Old Junction (the signalbox is on the left) it will move onto LNWR metals towards Arpley Junction. The Ship Canal is then crossed again by "Deviation No 3" (Latchford high-level bridge) on its way to Skelton Junction. *(J Lennon)*

Back on the Glazebrook to Godley Line, East from Skelton Junction

The section of line to the east, the Stockport, Timperley & Altrincham Railway, although authorized in 1861, actually opened on 1st December 1865. This was after the enabling Act of Parliament, the Cheshire Lines Transfer Act, was passed on 12th May 1865, which brought together a group of railway

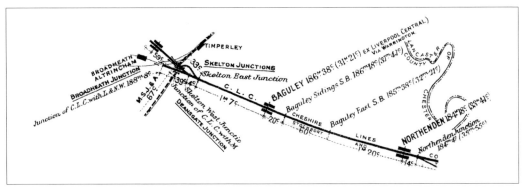

undertakings in Cheshire, and made the Great Northern Railway and the Manchester, Sheffield & Lincolnshire Railway the joint owners. The Act also allowed the Midland Railway to be a joint partner, which it became the next year.

Skelton Loop Line. Keeping its speed down to the regulation 15mph, with one of the daily hopper trains to Northwich, as it passes down from Skelton to Deansgate Junctions on 18th June, is Stanier 8F 2-8-0 48741. The concrete footbridge is interesting. With the initials CLR rather than CLC is the date – 1923. The company used both sets of initials without any discernable logic, and there is a similar example at Northwich. Replacing previous structures on the same site was this early ferro-concrete structure, similar to the one at Northwich. Many photographers used this as a vantage point. This bridge replaced a wooden one, locally known as "Black Bridge", which passed over the main running lines and the sidings, connecting up with the subway under the other four running lines. *(N Spilsbury)*

Skelton Loop Line, 1950. Heading up the gradient between Deansgate and Skelton Junctions is a train of mostly coal empties – ageing Pollit J10 class 0-6-0 65166 trundles past the well-tended allotments. How any work was done on them is a mystery with so many railway distractions! Not only is there this loop line, but across the picture is the main electrified line to Manchester. On the left, up on the viaduct, is the Cheshire Lines to Glazebrook. Trains from Manchester Piccadilly to Chester now use this loop line. *(N Spilsbury)*

Skelton Down Goods Loop, 1949. East of the rail junctions is the Moss Lane bridge and, about to pass under it, is LNER class B7 4-6-0 61710 on 23rd July. The 58-wagon down goods loop was very well used. The signalling arrangements are interesting. Over the main lines is a gantry with arms protecting the three exits from the junction, the taller post (for the West Timperley line) being the most important. At this time, all three routes have distant arms on the same post, indicating

the presence of another signalbox close by (west of Skelton Junction). For the Warrington line it is Broadheath No 1, while for the Skelton Loop line it is Deansgate Junction. Next to the up line are three small signals on one post. It was standard practice for trains going west to reverse out of the sidings, which was a tricky operation as trains became longer. The miniature arms then mirrored the ones on the gantry. *(N Spilsbury)*

East of Skelton Junction, 1960. Ferrying passengers to the Welsh coast is class 5 4-6-0 44846 on 7th August. Having departed from Sheffield Midland some two hours previously, it would be another two hours before the train arrived at Llandudno. There were two such trains in the 1951 timetable, both summer Saturdays only. The first left at 10.10am with the relief leaving half a hour later. They both stopped at Chinley, and then arrived here via Cheadle Heath. The brake van of an eastbound up freight train can just be made out. *(BKB Green)*

Skelton Junction, 1966. While the line is usually thought of as a freight line, it was also used by many passenger trains. They, like their freight counterparts, had no requirement to pass through Manchester, so were glad of this bypass route. On 9th July we see a summer Saturday-only train carrying the reporting number 1N85 passing east, having just left the junction. This train is the 11.45am from Llandudno to Newcastle. After picking up passengers at other

North Wales resorts like Colwyn Bay and Rhyl, it would next stop at Leeds City to change class 5 4-6-0 45446. To get there would involve the Cheshire Lines metals as far as Northenden Junction, and then the ex-LNWR lines. After passing through Stockport Edgeley, it would branch off at Heaton Norris Junction towards Guide Bridge. South of the station, at Denton Junction, it would swing east along the avoiding line through Hooley Hill and so to Stalybridge, where it went through Standedge tunnel to Huddersfield. Newcastle would be reached just after 6.30pm. *(P Hutchinson)*

East of Skelton Junction, 1967. While this area is generally depicted as an endless conveyor belt of coal trains for Liverpool docks, Partington Coal Basin and power stations along the way (as well as limestone trains for Northwich) the line did carry large amounts of non-coal freight too. In addition to the east to west trains, there was a similar level of traffic the other way, not only in empties, but also in oil products from the Cheshire refinery at Stanlow and Ellesmere Port to Yorkshire. Some

trains were so heavy that double-heading was the order of the day. It is hard to look at this picture without sensing the immense power of these locomotives as they burst under the bridge. Was "train driver" one of the jobs that this trio aspired to? What were their thoughts and comments to each other as this display of power passed their way? Ex-Crosti-boilered 9F 92025 pilots 92048 on 1st July. The signal is for the down main line, with a bracket for the loop. *(N Spilsbury)*

East of Skelton Junction, 1966. As well as around 11 freight trains an hour passing along this section of line, it was extensively used by Saturdays-only holiday traffic. Sporting code 1N82 (9.15am SO Leeds City to Llandudno, arriving at 12.50pm) is Standard class "Britannia" pacific 70009 *Alfred the Great* on 30th July. It was built at Crewe in 1951 with a type 1 tender (7 tons of coal and 4,250 gallons of water) which had a recess to allow better visibility when running tender first – not that it did so that

often, being chiefly used on express passenger trains rather than mixed traffic, for which they were designed. Following an accident at Didcot in 1955, the view from the cab was improved by removing the handrails on the smoke deflectors and replacing them with six hand-holes. The AWS apparatus beneath the buffer beam is protected from damage from the coupling by a steel plate. Shed 12A was Carlisle (Kingsmoor), and it has been cared for in a manner typical of certain ex-LMS sheds in that area, with various parts of the front of the engine in a light colour – probably pale (Caledonian) blue. *(N Spilsbury)*

Baguley Station, Exterior, 1910. It is hard for us to imagine a car-free station these days. For about 90 of the years it was open, little changed at Baguley, and it was only in the last years of opening that the railway's transport monopoly was challenged. A new station is believed to be on the cards for Timperley along with one at Cheadle. The former would be approximately ½ mile west of the original (Baguley) station, behind the library, with access from both the Stockport and Park Roads. However, local residents have objected, and the matter has been "on hold" since April 1997. *(Stations UK)*

Baguley, 1964. Viewed on the day passenger services were withdrawn, 30th November, we see the small shelter on the island platform and the main station buildings, opened in 1866, which were to be templates for the company's main line between Manchester and Liverpool, opened in 1873. Heading towards Skelton Junction is Stanier 8F 2-8-0 48249 with a load of limestone from Tunstead quarry to the ICI works at Winnington near Northwich. *(BWL Brooksbank)*

Baguley, 1949. This was typical of the four passenger trains (six on Saturdays) that stopped here post-war. LNER J39s had sufficient power and pace to haul the all-stations trains from Stockport Tiviot Dale to Liverpool Central, a journey that would take 90 minutes. On 15th August 64723 has its new owner's name on its tender. One problem with timing involved the use of non-corridor stock. For each carriage there were

a large number of doors to close, and this could only be done at the speed of the station staff walking along the platform. Even a small undertaking as Baguley gave employment to at least four people (all male), one of which in pre-Grouping times was Mr John Williams, the station master. At the south of the station was a loop and a small goods yard. *(Ray Hinton)*

Baguley, 1956. Passing east under Brook's Drive bridge with a train of empty hopper wagons on 25th May is Stanier 8F 2-8-0 48045. The road bridge was built in 1870, after the railway was built, and the diamond sign on the right abutment gives notice about the safe weight limit on the bridge. The fancy barge-boards on the station buildings show up well, as do their supports. Of interest is the handcart, parked at the end of the

building ready for use, and the sign under the canopy, which reads, "Ladies waiting room", illustrating the kind of lavatorial facilities that today's train companies are unwilling to re-introduce despite Government exhortation. Looking west, the gradient can clearly be seen. Having been on a rise since just after Skelton Junction, the section we see is 1 in 75, with some respite through the station on the level. *(Peter Hutchinson)*

Baguley, around 1912. Views of the station from the road bridge looking west are not very common. An eastbound train is expected, as the signalman has pulled lever no 23 to bring the easily-visible signal to the off position to allow the train to proceed. Note how even the space under the steps to the footbridge has been utilized as a storage room. Two private owner wagons are in the small goods yard with, probably its staple traffic, coal. One such merchant was Mr George Hankinson, who had a yard at Orchard Place in Timperley. In the bottom right is the controlling signalbox at Baguley Station. This replacement

box opened in 1876, and its 24 levers were (unusually for the company) in a brick building. The elaborate bargeboard has had a piece trimmed from the left-hand end, presumably to protect staff when cleaning the windows perched on the ledge. An ornate gas lamp would illuminate the only means of identification on the island platform, and there were two other such lamps at the western end. *(Lens of Sutton)*

East of Baguley, 1958. With rail access on the down side was the Wythenshawe works of Metropolitan Vickers, now part of Roundthorn Industrial Estate, to the south of the line. There were two loops accessed by trailing connections from the main lines, and released electrically from Baguley signalbox. LNER class O4/8 2-8-0 63573 passes west *(above)* with a mixed, partially-fitted, freight train. Preparing to stop at Baguley station *(below)* is the 3.17pm from Stockport Tiviot Dale; Warrington is its destination. The nine-station trip would take just over 40 minutes, and adequate motive power is provided by Fairburn 2-6-4T 42183 on 16th September. Today, six coaches would be a long train, but in those days it was nothing extraordinary. *(Both, Peter Hutchinson)*

Northenden Station, 1952. An excursion heading west has just passed through Northenden station on 26th July. On the right is the small goods yard, complete with four-ton crane; the scene is reminiscent of Glazebrook. The large boiler of K3 class 2-6-0 61865 shows up well. The reporting number was for a New Mills to Southport train, mostly on Cheshire Lines metals. Its journey would be to Glazebrook and then onto the Liverpool to Manchester main line. At Halewood, it would pass north, through Aintree and on to Southport Lord Street. *(BKB Green)*

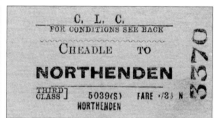

Northenden Station, 1952. A not-too-wide-awake passenger could be forgiven for mistaking this station for Baguley, as the main buildings are very similar. To drum up more trade, the station has had "for Wythenshawe" added. We are looking out of a window watching a train departing for Stockport – our platform had a small waiting room. *(HC Casserley)*

Northenden Station, 1952. About to enter the station tender first, is a stopping train from Stockport with Stanier 2-6-2T 40094 in charge; its home shed was 9F, Heaton Mersey. Note the tall bracket signal on the wrong side, for sighting purposes, the arms being operated by levers 20 and 21. Intensive as the line was, the station saw only a handful of stopping trains each way per day, so the staff had plenty of time to tend to the garden at the end of the down platform. *(BPC)*

Northenden Station, 1976. There are several tall signalboxes on the route from Godley to Glazebrook, all of a different design. At Apethorne, it was built of stone, and at Skelton of wood, while here, bricks were used. Perhaps it illustrates the different influence of different railway companies on the line. Here, the original line (Stockport, Timperley & Altrincham) was authorized before the LNWR wanted this to become a junction. They therefore probably had to pay for its erection, hence the fancy pattern of the locking-room windows. It must have been an arduous task getting coal, etc, all the way up to the cabin. *(ND Mundy)*

Northenden Junction, 1948. Heading west is a local train, probably bound for Liverpool, hauled by LNER 4-4-0 2321 on 27th April as seen from Longley Lane bridge; a similar view would have been obtained from the adjacent signalbox. One role of signalmen was to log the passage of trains along the line. Good visibility was essential to do this, hence the elevated position relative to the road bridge. This box is still open. *(JD Darby)*

Northenden Junction, 1949. Looking east from the overbridge, this view shows Stanier 8F 8329 passing west with a load of limestone in hopper wagons. It will have joined the Glazebrook to Godley line just over a mile to the east at Cheadle Junction on a spur down from the ex-MR line. The Cheshire Lines' habit of putting signals on tall lattice posts is illustrated well here. Waiting on the ex-LNWR line to the right is a sister loco with another freight train. The section of line from Northenden Junction to Skelton Junction must have been one of the most heavily-used freight lines in the country. *(Ray Hinton)*

Northenden, 1902. A fascinating insight into a world of only a hundred years ago. In Pellon Mews, there was a dwelling and shed belonging to Wallace Wright, who acted as a goods receiving agent for the railway company and (as can be seen in the shed) provided a horse-drawn taxi service for passengers. As there was a crossing of the River Mersey a short distance east at Cheadle, it is not surprising that the district was mentioned in the Domesday Book of 1086 as part of the salt road from Cheshire to Manchester. Until 1931, Northenden had been able to retain its identity, but with the Wythenshaw development it became part of the city. Motorway interchanges dominate the area now. *(J Ryan Collection)*

Connections with the LNWR

With the north to south line through Stockport opening in the early 1840s, it was always likely that its lines would link up with the Glazebrook to Godley line that passed beneath it twenty years later. Connections via Guide Bridge had established the area as a cross-Pennine route that could avoid Manchester on the way to Liverpool. The line from Northenden Junction to Edgeley Junction enabled this to happen.

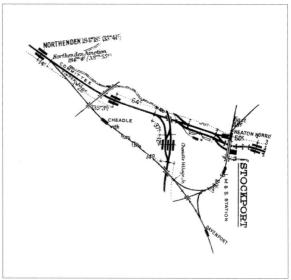

Cheadle Station Exterior, 1910. The LNWR line from Stockport to Northenden Junction crossed over the main turnpike road to Manchester, opening on 1st August 1866. The fine two-storey building has pretty brickwork above the windows, and the hoarding announces the railway company and some of the destinations that could be reached. Under the bridge was a terrace of houses including the Railway Inn, next door to which lived a railway porter named Herbert Hamer, with colleague, Ben Sutclife, next-door-but-one. *(Stations UK)*

Cheadle Station Interior, c.1900. As the railway is on an embankment, the external two-storey building becomes single-storey at platform level. In 1905, the suffix "South" was added to its name, but as with many other stations, it closed on 1st January 1917 for some of the Great War, never to reopen. Entering from the east is one of the typical services to Broadheath in the west. From there, connections could be made to Warrington (Arpley) and Liverpool. A short-lived service from Buxton to Liverpool started in the 1880s. Slater's Directory lists William Gardom as stationmaster, and in the small goods yard to the north and west of the station, the coal merchants, Benjamin Sutclife, Ryecroft Brothers, James Grime and A&W Tonge. The latter pair lived next to the police station on the Stockport Road while Mr Grime lived just a few doors to the east. *(BPC)*

Cheadle Village, 1966. Needing all the experience that the two drivers have is a loaded coal train coming down the 1 in 68 gradient towards Northenden junction. I wonder how many lads watched trains like this going past from their bedroom windows. Residents have a good view of a brace of Stanier 8Fs, 48634 and 48334, on 20th August. *(Locofotos)*

Cheadle Village, 1965. Pausing while taking a trainload of full coal wagons west is Stanier 8F 2-8-0 48338. A piece of leather tubing feeds water from the parachute tank to the tender, and is operated by the rope attached to the lever. In the foreground are the remains of a recently-lifted pair of loops. The box in the background is Cheadle Village Junction.

Cheadle Village, early 1960s. Looking east, this view shows the line to Edgeley Junction going straight on with that to Buxton on the right. Looking like double-track, there was only a single line connection from here to Davenport Junction, the line to the left being a long siding. The 25-lever signalbox controlled the junction and commencement of the single line section and also the two loops off to the right with some wagons in them.

Cheadle Village, 1963. East of Cheadle the LNWR line curves north to meet the main line at Edgeley Junction. At that point there are two junctions, one to the east (Northenden) and the other to the west (Hazel Grove). However, prior to this in 1884, the company built a connection between these two lines to make a triangle. This short section crosses the line that the other two branch from. Convenient as it was, small sections of line like this were built with little regard to gradients, nearby Edgeley shed providing additional power. The gradient is well shown by this Birkenhead to Buxton freight on 12th February. "Crab" 2-6-0 42813 *(upper)* hauls a very long train, while Stanier 8F 2-8-0 No 48062 *(lower)* acts as banker. When the turntable at Manchester London Road was removed in early 1958, it posed a problem as Pacific engines could not be turned. The up "Comet" (15 coaches on a Friday night) was to be hauled by a Pacific that had arrived earlier that day from Crewe, so to turn it round, it was sent via Edgeley No 1 towards Hazel Grove, then over this line towards Cheadle Village Junction, and reversed again to arrive at Edgeley No 2. Thence it ran to Longsight shed to be prepared for the 5.45pm to the capital. *(Both Gordon Coltas Trust)*

Edgeley Junction, 1966. The line from Edgeley Junction to Northenden not only saw numerous freight trains avoiding Manchester, but also many passenger trains. Here, probably with a train for North Wales, is Jubilee class 4-6-0 45647 *Sturdee* about to pass under Stockholm Road bridge. On the right is Edgeley No 1 box, which controls the departure of the line to Buxton from the main line. Trains for Chester, which used to depart from Manchester Central, now depart hourly from Piccadilly, taking five minutes less than they did 50 years ago. After a trip to Stockport they now pass along the line this train is on, to arrive at Altrincham, and thence all stations to Chester. *(T Lewis)*

Edgeley Junction, c.1966. Leaving the main line to Crewe and skirting Edgeley engine shed is an oil train, probably for Stanlow refinery on the Manchester Ship Canal opposite Runcorn. Notice the practice of inserting a couple of wagons between the steam engine and the oil tankers to reduce the risk of fire. Standard class 9F 2-10-0 92094 puts up a lot of smoke as it sets off west. Edgeley No 1 signalbox peers above the oil tankers, and an electric locomotive is hiding behind the wagons on the right. *(G Harrop)*

Edgeley, 1967. Whilst waiting for a pathway, the firemen of the engines take the opportunity to shovel the coal forward. The Stanlow to Leeds oil train will need all the power of two Standard class 9F 2-10 0 engines 92109 and 92029 to move the heavy train up to Standedge tunnel and through the Pennines. The train is on the up Liverpool line and will soon pass round Edgeley station, to cross the viaduct to Heaton Norris Junction. It looks as if the return working is on the down line. On the right, Stockport shed is in its death throes, closing the next year. The two people watching could combine two of life's great pleasures at the same place – the local football team, and now Sale Sharks rugby club are just a stone's throw behind them. *(G Coltas Trust)*

Edgeley No 2. A wonderful picture, soon to be swept away by "modernisation". Curving in from the left are the pair of lines that originated at Northenden Junction, and arrived here from Cheadle Junction. A quarter of a mile south along the main line to Crewe is the junction (No 1) with the line east from Buxton. Looking north along the main quadruple main lines, we see the line to Northenden and the engine shed is curving away behind the signalbox. With 54 levers, it is one of the smallest on the line in this vicinity. Its partner, No 1 box, has 90 levers while those at either end of the station have a massive 135 levers each. All these structures survived the turmoil of electrification in the early 1960s, and still exist today. *(G Harrop)*

Mersey Square, 1950. Across the background is the LNWR viaduct over the River Mersey with Edgeley's canopy just visible on the left. The bridge carries Wellington Road over the river, with Mersey Square in the foreground. The tram is for Cheadle Heath, and it was the ability of such vehicles to penetrate housing developments that caused the demise of suburban railway services. Behind us, at the corner of High Street and St Peter's Gate was an office for the firm of Dean, Henry & Pearson who were travel agents, from 1878. The GCR bought the firm as Dean & Dawson, and by this time the MR were associated with Thomas Cook & Son. *(JH Meredith)*

Heaton Norris Junction, 1951. Looking north from Bowerfold Lane, this view suggests that the signalman has been busy. Next to the box, on the up fast line, is one of Fowler's 2-6-4T engines, 42398, probably slowing down to stop at the station a short distance ahead. Bringing a class H freight train off the branch, is LNWR class G2a 0-8-0 49355. It will continue along the up slow line. The line on the extreme right feeds the adjacent goods warehouse. What an exciting place the dwelling on the right would have been to have lived in! *(T Lewis)*

Heaton Norris Goods Depot, 1964. Fed by the lines from Jubilee sidings on the branch is this magnificent 1882 brick warehouse accessed from Wellington Road. The name of its owners is proudly written in white bricks across the top for all to see. It is now a Grade 2 listed building, currently used as a furniture store. How such places operated is illustrated by the goings-on in the foreground. Wagons would be shunted into the adjacent sidings, usually by a "Jinty" tank engine, but horses frequently were used. There they would be unloaded, or by means of ropes, turntables and a capstan, turned and taken into the building for unloading. BR was a "common carrier", which meant that it was obliged to carry anything to anywhere a customer wanted. Road traffic had the same restriction, but hauliers could decline to carry some goods, saying that they weren't specialized to do so. Would the country's railways have survived competition better if both had been governed by the same rules? Being placed onto the trailer of a three-wheel "mechanical horse" are some wooden crates of different shapes and sizes. The crane assists, but it is taking four men to do this job, illustrating how hopelessly uncompetitive rail was. Further along the warehouse is the covered trailer for the Scammell driving unit. *(R Essery)*

Jubilee Sidings, 1965. Round the corner, under Wellington Road, the quadruple branch fed Jubilee sidings, opened in 1899. Looking north towards Stalybridge this view shows the main lines towards the left of the picture. The sidings consisted of fifteen loops and as a pair of additional goods lines. An unidentified Stanier 8F 2-8-0 is probably in the middle of operations here. In the distance are some coal wagons on the up goods line. It looks as if the train had been "cut" with several wagons having been deposited nearest to us. The engine may well be going back to retrieve its discarded wagons or to collect some others from the sidings. *(J Fairclough)*

Jubilee Sidings, 1935.
Probably waiting for a pathway across the viaduct is the crew of Prince of Wales class 4-6-0 25044 *King of Italy*. In the centre is the 40-lever signalbox; it had no responsibility for the main lines. The signalman's job was to control movements to the sidings and to the lines feeding the warehouse that led back next to the main lines at Heaton Norris junction. Access to the up slow line there was controlled by the junction box. *(BPC)*

Ash Bridge, 1963. Heading west is a fitted freight along the up slow line. Having originated in Mirfield (L&YR) it will have passed through the Standedge tunnels (LNWR), flirted with Guide Bridge (GCR) and will likely proceed onto our line. It is signalled, by the raised arm on the right, to pass onto the up goods line where, no doubt, it will await a pathway across the magnificent Grade II listed viaduct, at Stockport. *(G Coltas Trust)*

Ash Bridge, 1960s. Just over 1,000 yards from the junction with the main line is the north-eastern access point to the sidings. The 43-lever wooden box had a long life, existing from 1899 until 1977. The signals for the up lines are on this superb gantry. The pair of posts nearest to us are for the slow line, and the other three for the fast line. For each set, the tallest post indicates the most commonly used route, but note the provision of two smaller "calling-on" arms. Passing along one of the down lines is a train of oil tankers, probably from Stanlow. It will have traversed the section of the Cheshire Lines route from Skelton Junction to Northenden Junction, with a probable destination in West Yorkshire, for example, Yamm Lane, Leeds. *(BPC)*

Back on the Glazebrook to Godley line from Cheadle

Cheadle, 1939. A typical three-coach stopping train has just left the station on its route west towards Glazebrook. Already getting on for forty years old is LNER J10 class 0-6-0 5174 on a fine July day with the outbreak of war less than two months away. At the rear of the cab is a roll of tarpaulin, which would be very useful when heavy rain occurred. To the right of the down train is the long headshunt for the small goods yard, which had a crane that could lift 1½ tons. There was also a facility for loading horseboxes. Manchester Road bridge is in the background. *(CM & JM Bentley)*

Cheadle, 1959. With the time approximately 6.45pm on 20th June, a train heads west from Cheadle station. It would have left Stockport Tiviot Dale at 6.23pm, and will stop at all stations, via Widnes, to Liverpool Central. A five-coach train was a respectable challenge for Stanier 2-6-4T 42580, but as the platform here could only accommodate three coaches, and this was non-corridor stock, two attempts were necessary, which all added to the time. *(Ray Hinton)*

Cheadle, 1948. Hoping to get punters there in time for the first race is an express for the Grand National meeting on 20th March. Avoiding Manchester is an excursion from Luton with pilot engine, LMS 4-4-0 2P 632, and train engine, "Crab" 2-6-0 2839, hauling thirteen coaches. The pilot will most probably have been picked up at Godley. Having just passed through Cheadle station, the Cheshire Lines lower-quadrant signal is on the wrong side to assist sighting as the line here curves gently under a road and the Styal line railway bridge. *(HD Bowtell/J Ryan Collection)*

Cheadle, 1939. Racing through on the down line is an express for Liverpool from Hull hauled by a LNER Atlantic 4-4-2 4420. Probably very little had changed since the line opened on 1st December 1865, the station opening within the following two months. Slightly north of the line is the Towers, a large house built at the same time as the line opened. It was there that a group of businessmen were invited by the then owner, Daniel Adamson, on 27th June 1882. The topic of their discussion was, "The possibility of constructing a ship canal between Manchester and the coast, and so rendering Manchester independent of Liverpool for its imports and exports." The ultimate outcome was the Manchester Ship Canal Company. *(BPC)*

Cheadle, 1939. From the late 1920s until 1931 steam railcars were used on the Altrincham to Stockport Tiviot Dale service, being known locally as the, "Baguley Bus". The Cheshire Lines Railway, as Britain's premier joint line, had distinctive wagons, carriages and signals, but they never owned locomotives, hiring them instead from the constituent companies. However, they did buy a number of steam railcars like the chocolate and buff No 600 seen here. Unlike those used on the LNER, these never carried names. The idea behind railcars was to attract more passengers, and in some areas (around Southport, for example) extra

"Motor Halts" were built wherever the line crossed a road. In other places, an increased frequency resulted, but the thinking here was to reduce costs to compete with bus services. Over time, the maintenance bills increased, so their advantages were lost. The footplate staff complained about conditions, so they earned the nickname "sweat boxes". It, and its three sisters were stored at Old Trafford, late in 1941, never to work again. *(BPC)*

Cheadle, 1949. I wonder what the young boy, short trousers and shirt collar over his jacket, is thinking as he watches the freight train head west. Getting the right of way from the fine upper-quadrant Cheshire Lines signals is ex-LNER J11 65209 on 3rd July. The wagons carry loads that needed protection from the weather, so they have tarpaulin sheets over them. The shelter on the Stockport platform, nameplate, signalbox and upper-quadrant signals all show up well. Note how the down loop was accessed from the main lines. *(N Preedy)*

Cheadle, Exterior, 1946. As part of the Stockport, Timperley & Altrincham Railway, Northenden and Baguley stations were from the same mould. It was deemed to be a successful one, as the same design was used several years later for many of the stations of the now Cheshire Lines main line between Liverpool and Manchester. An adapted plan is always cheaper than an original one. The notice boards are clearly labelled, "LMS" and "CLR". Less than half a mile south, and much closer to the village centre, was the LNWR station. *(Stations UK)*

Cheadle. Writers usually pay a good deal of attention to the main buildings at stations, and the humble shelter is often ignored. Standing on the up, Stockport, platform is a structure that many stations would be proud of today. Built of brick, it has a seat and many posters advertising railway services – all from a pre-graffiti age. Milepost 35 is interesting – the distance is from Liverpool and there would have been a capital letter 'M' above the number in earlier days. These were compulsory after an Act of Parliament in 1845, and had to be every quarter of a mile along the line so that a train's speed could be calculated. Mileposts and the station clock were essential when running a timetable. However, it wasn't until 1884 that local time was abandoned everywhere, and GMT adopted instead. Looking remarkably like the stationmaster's house is the building in the background. *Slater's Directory* for 1919 lists Horace G Howell as stationmaster, James Broughton as platelayer and Samuel Bickerton as signalman. North of here is the flood plain of the River Mersey until Cheadle Bridge is reached. For centuries, this was one of the few crossing places of the river, and Cheadle, being mentioned in the Domesday book, was more important than Stockport. The bridge was rebuilt to lift the road above the river's flood level in 1852. *(RK Blencowe)*

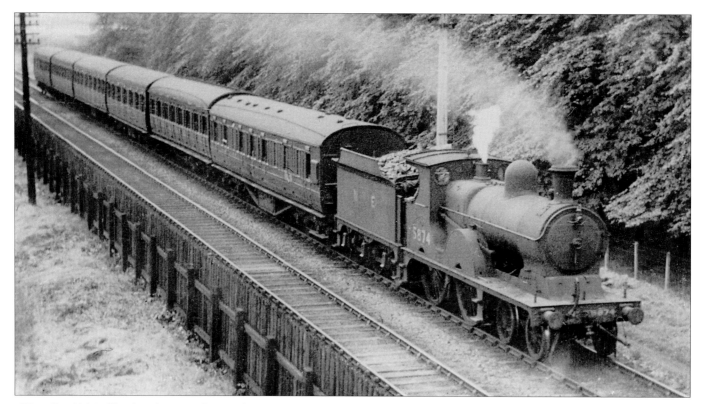

Cheadle, 1945. Slowing down, and preparing to stop at the station the other side of the bridge that this picture was taken from, is a stopping train from Stockport bound for Liverpool. Only a handful of such trains stopped here, augmented by a couple more on Saturdays. The engine is of MS&LR vintage from 1899, classified by the GCR as 11A 874. The LNER made it class D6 5874 from 1924, and it was withdrawn in 1947 after carrying the number 2106 for just a year. *(BPC)*

Cheadle West, 1952. In need of a coat of paint is the 20-lever box half a mile from Cheadle station. Its purpose is to control access from a set of loops on the down side on the right, as well as being a block post for the main line. While the signals for the train are upper-quadrant ones, those to allow egress from the sidings are of the lower-quadrant type. The two coaches of a Liverpool-bound stopping train will not tax 2-6-2T 40203, one of a handful of engines that the LMS rebuilt with larger boilers in 1941. *(N Preedy Collection)*

Cheadle Exchange Sidings, 1956. Looking west from the steps of the signalbox, this view shows the set of sidings built at the opening of the curve in 1902, to facilitate the exchange of wagons between the Cheshire Lines and the Midland Railway. The connections to the running lines are interesting. The sidings have a trailing link to the up (Stockport) line and a line from the Liverpool curve in the down direction. Dominating the scene are the two tall wooden signal posts, for the up main on the right and for the down loop in the middle of the picture. To the left of the picture are the filter beds for Stockport's sewage works completed in 1882, next to huts for bicycles and cabins for workers. *(Signalling Record Society, Scrimgeour Collection)*

Cheadle Junction, 1956. Looking towards Stockport this time we see the typical Cheshire Lines signalbox with 32 levers. White is the colour of the wooden vertical cladding and of the letters on a black background for the nameboard. These sidings were obviously well used judging by the provision of gas lights for staff to walk on the trackside footpath; they closed in 1971. The River Mersey is to the left at a lower level. *(Signalling Record Society, Scrimgeour Collection)*

Cheadle Junction, 1954. The photographer has walked about a quarter of a mile east towards Stockport, crossed the River Mersey, and is looking back the way he has come. The couple in the foreground take a July stroll by the river, oblivious to the rail activity up above. Cheadle Junction signalbox is controlling the movements of two trains. In the background is an up train of empty coal wagons that has left the exchange sidings, and is starting the climb up towards Cheadle Heath station. Going the opposite way with loaded coal wagons is LNER class O4/6 2-8-0 63862 probably on its way towards Glazebrook and then Liverpool's docks. *(Ray Hinton)*

Mersey Bridge No 72, 1950s. In the background are the signals and box at Cheadle Junction. Heading east is a freight train with an unidentified engine, most probably an O4 class 2-8-0. Judging by the position of the signal arms on the lattice post, it is preparing to stop. On the other side of the three squares on the brackets are small red arms, which will be easily visible to train crews, as the square is painted white behind them. *(Ray Hinton)*

Liverpool Curve, 1953. The complex bridge arrangements are shown up well. Not only does the Cheshire Lines cross the River Mersey, but it is crossed by this lattice girder bridge carrying the Midland Railway's final attempt to enter central Manchester. Heading west across the Mersey along the Cheshire Lines route to Liverpool is ex-LMS Compound 4-4-0 41118 on 22nd May. It has just gone under the MR Disley cut, which itself is about to pass over the Mersey as the river turns through 90° here. Joining the two lines, behind the photographer, is the Liverpool Curve. *(Ray Hinton)*

Cheadle Junction, 1968. Almost at the end of steam we see Stanier 8F 48252 pulling a trainload of coal wagons west on 16th February. The photographer was standing almost on top of the point rodding of Cheadle Junction box. The signal post to the left not only controlled the main line, but also the access to sidings to the left and to Heaton Mersey loco shed to the right. The plume of smoke in the background is from an engine there, and the roof visible over the bridge is the coaling stage, which is presumably the destination of the two men walking with their backs to any train on their track; they are just crossing the River Mersey. The bridge in the background carries the former Midland Railway line from New Mills South Junction, through Disley tunnel to Chorlton Junction, then on Cheshire Lines metals into Central Station. Off to the right is the Liverpool Curve which joined the MR line at Cheadle Heath Station. *(BPC)*

Connections to the Midland Railway

One of the prime targets for the Midland Railway was Manchester, but what a struggle it had to achieve this goal! After being ousted from London Road, the company practiced the trickle-down approach, and by passing over other lines, including the Cheshire Lines of which it was a partner, it could arrive at a new Central station. This and the Stockport avoiding line meant that they could compete with the LNWR for Manchester traffic.

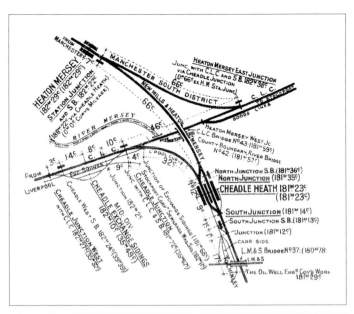

Manchester Central Station, 1966. Having arrived, the MR stamped its mark in style with its imposing Central station, now the G-Mex Centre. While it wasn't the first major station in the town (that was London Road) nor the biggest (Victoria) nor even the last (Exchange), it was certainly the most magnificent. The single span roof is spectacular, and the sheer scale made it a worthy contender for "Gateway to the capital". The ironwork for the imposing 210ft arch roof is shown off well, and the girders continue well below platform level to create an undercroft that was used as an extension of the goods depot. From here, the Midland Railway used part of the Glazebrook to Godley section for services to Yorkshire, and the Cheshire Lines Railway also operated its "Punctual" service every hour to Liverpool. Class 5 4-6-0 45392 waits with a parcels train while the station enjoys a revival in trains due to the rebuilding of London Road. This scene showing a diesel train arriving with an express would be soon extinguished as Piccadilly rose from the ashes of London Road. *(HB Priestley, Collection of W Taylor)*

Deansgate Goods Depot, no date. In the background is the massive warehouse opened by the Great Northern Railway on 1st July 1898 with its connection to the passenger lines just off to the left. As one of the original partners of the Cheshire Lines Railway, the Great Northern was able to penetrate this Lancashire stronghold. From this warehouse, its trains passed onto the Glazebrook to Godley section to access their own lines east of the Pennines. To the right is the shape of what was left of the Cheshire Lines goods shed accessed from tracks behind the coaches. Setting out past an adapted MR water column is LMS 4P compound 4-4-0 41188. Within about half a mile were the equally massive goods undertakings of the LNWR at Liverpool Road, and just across the River Irwell was the L&Y at Salford. *(BKB Green)*

Manchester Central, 1928. The real revenue earner for railways was freight, hence the development of goods facilities next to the passenger station. Apart from the goods operated from the extensive undercroft at Central, there were two massive goods depots in the vicinity. North-west of the station, bounded by Watson and Windmill Streets, was the site of one such building. Notice that the wording is an extra to the building, not like at Warrington or Brunswick, where it is in carved stone. Also, there is no attempt to explain who the owners of the Cheshire Lines are. One can almost hear the horses' hooves as they emerge from the numbered arches into Watson Street to deliver all over the city. During World War II, the building was hit by a bomb, and the top floor effectively became the roof! *(Manchester City Engineers Archive)*

Trafford Park, 1947. While the main passenger lines that the MR ran over were to Manchester Central, connections at Throstle Nest Junction allowed trains to turn east onto the main Cheshire Lines route to Liverpool. After a short distance along these lines past United's football ground, with the engine shed as a neighbour, the industries alongside the Ship Canal are reached. Adjacent is the Trafford Park Estate with its numerous international clients, many rail-connected, with the Ship Canal forming two boundaries and the Bridgewater Canal the remaining pair. Something like 50,000 people worked in this vast industrial estate, with half as many again during World War II. LNER 4-6-0 class B9 1477 (formerly 6113) waits by the parachute water tank with a covered van. *(HC Casserley)*

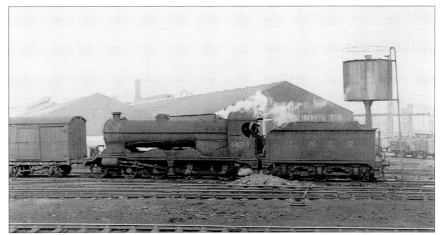

Trafford Park, 1957. An Act of 1904 enabled the operating company to extend the railway to new premises without the need to go to Parliament each time. One such firm that took advantage of the good transport connections offered was Brown & Polson Ltd. It purchased this 1929-built Barclay 0-4-0ST to shunt in its premises, and the engine is seen here waiting by the side of Trafford Park Road. While this may seen as a quaint light railway serving a few factories, that would be to underestimate the importance of this area, as in 1931, it was estimated that 3% of the nation's railway tonnage was moved over Trafford Park's system, with the factories consuming a colossal 300,000 tons of coal annually. *(N Jones/GK Fox Collection)*

Heaton Mersey Station, 1939. From 1873, the Cheshire Lines had routes from Manchester Central to Liverpool Central, from Glazebrook to Godley and others south of Altrincham. Such was the Midland Railway's desire to gain access Manchester that their chairman for many years, JJ Allport, said that the quest was to be undertaken, "whatever the cost". Having paid for an enlarged London Road (a station shared with three other companies) the MR was given three years notice to quit in 1875, which is why the MR supported the Manchester South District Railway when the other

partners in the CLR dropped out – firstly the GNR and then the MS&LR. The plan was to build an almost six-mile line from Cornbrook (on the main CLR route to Liverpool) to Heaton Mersey (on the CLR from Glazebrook to Godley). A station opened here just north of the River Mersey in 1880, and this view is south with the junction signals standing out clearly. Trains would pass from here to connect to the Cheshire Lines route to Stockport Tiviot Dale station by the left-hand route. Outwardly the buildings resemble a stretched version of Baguley, Cheadle, Northenden or several others along the CLR main line between Liverpool and Manchester. The other three stations on the line both had extensive canopies for passengers' protection. A footpath went across the line, hence the extension to left-hand end of the footbridge, just visible behind the station buildings. The up platform has a brick shelter with quite a large canopy from it. *(Stations UK)*

Heaton Mersey Station, around the late 1920s. With the opening of Manchester Central station in 1877, the Midland Railway was able to achieve entry to "Cottonopolis", at last, in 1880. However, its services to London, although competitive in terms of scenery, were not in terms of time. The sinuous pathway with many junctions, steep gradients and slow running left them at a disadvantage. Consequently, typical of an age which brimmed with confidence, the company decided to build its own high-speed link. This involved a junction at New Mills, some 17 miles south of the city, bypassing Stockport to the west, and

joining the Manchester South District lines here at Heaton Mersey. This was the Disley Cut-off, opened in 1902. The junction here was by the end of the station and necessitated a severe (15mph) speed restriction for trains passing along the original line to join the Glazebrook to Godley line. Unfortunately, a failure to adhere to the restriction led to this derailment. Looking south, this view shows the signalbox having a lucky escape and the tall signals, right for the cut-off and left for the original line. As a consequence, the whole junction was moved a short distance south and the speed limit was raised. On the right is the goods yard. *(Stockport Libraries)*

Heaton Mersey Curve 1954. After passing through Heaton Mersey station, the South District line curved east and descended to join the line from Glazebrook at Heaton Mersey East Junction. BR Standard class 2-6-0 78023 brings a stopping train, probably from Sheffield, up the gradient controlled by lower-quadrant signals towards Heaton Mersey Station Junction. Interestingly, the MR ordered 40 6-wheel coaches in 1883, and twenty years later, finding increasing demand for its services, brought in seven rakes of nine coaches for the South District trains. Each train would have provided 528 seats (168 First and 360 Third). Originally illuminated by gas, they were converted to electric lighting by the LMS. *(Ray Hinton)*

Heaton Mersey Curve, 1952. Heading up the 1 in 172 incline from the Cheshire Lines to Heaton Mersey station is this stopping passenger train. Ivatt 2-6-2T 41246 has just passed the signal post whose arms were operated by two different boxes. The top (stop) arm was worked by lever no 15 in Heaton Mersey East junction, while the lower (distant) arm is worked by lever no 26 in Heaton Mersey Station Junction box. As the land here is almost "green belt" between Manchester and Stockport, patronage of the station was far less than its neighbours. With today's congested access to central Manchester, one wonders whether such a service, along with "Park 'n' Ride" from Cheadle Heath, would now be invaluable.
(Norman Preedy Collection)

The Midland Railway Bridges Nos 42 & 43, 1952. Heading towards Heaton Mersey station is a down train, probably empty stock judging by the length of the train. While it will not be a problem for the engine (Stanier 2-6-2T 40118) to get the train started, it will require skill from the footplate crew to keep it moving at a reasonable speed. The second and third coaches are passing over the Cheshire Lines (bridge No 43), and the later coaches are passing over the River Mersey (No 42). The fine MR lower-quadrant signals show up well. *(Ray Hinton)*

Cheadle Heath North Junction, circa late 1950s. Having left Heaton Mersey station a few minutes ago, and crossed both the CLR and the River Mersey, this stopping train is passing from one set of lines to the other. Many services from Manchester Central terminated here. In the 40-lever wooden signalbox, lever No 37 has been pulled to indicate which platform the train is to go to. Levers 30 and 31 will also have to be pulled in Cheadle Heath North box to allow access to the platforms. Stanier 2-6-2T 40124 is obeying the imposing bracket signal, and is preparing to stop at Cheadle Heath station, some 200 yards in front. The two lines on the left form the "Liverpool Curve" down to meet the Cheshire Lines metals at Cheadle Junction. *(BPC)*

Cheadle Heath North, 1961. This tank train has probably come from Stanlow oil refinery on the banks of the River Mersey, almost at the western end of the Manchester Ship Canal. An unidentified Standard 2-10-0 is lead by MR 4F 0-6-0 44250 in August. They have dragged their load up the 1 in 68 gradient from the Cheshire Lines along the 700-yard Liverpool Curve to this point. In the background can be made out the bridge over the Cheshire Lines by the other pair of lines here, on the right. The signals the train is obeying are of the upper-quadrant variety, sandwiched in between the elevated bracket signal on the right and the facing post on the left, both lower-quadrants. *(N Preedy Collection)*

Cheadle Heath, around 1960. Opening on 1st October 1901 as Cheadle Heath Midland, the station became "for Stockport" after only seven months, but the "for" was removed in October 1908. Basically, there were four through platforms and an up bay, all connected by a covered footbridge to the station buildings on the left. Two platforms were on the main line (the "Manchester" platforms, on the left) and two were on the branch that met the CLR (the "Liverpool" ones, on the right). On each platform was a brick building housing the facilities needed, such as toilets and waiting room. Common uses of the right-hand platforms were for local stopping trains and for freight, either on their way to Liverpool, or to Manchester but waiting for a faster moving train to overtake. A coal train is passing under our position on Stockport Road as we look south. On the right is the large imposing goods shed with the extensive goods yard behind it. British Railways removed the "Stockport" suffix in June 1965, and all the passenger trains 18 months later. *(Stockport Libraries)*

Cheadle Heath South Junction, 1951.
Looking north we see the freight facilities.
The main pair of lines are to the right with the
up bay on the extreme right. Stanier 8F 2-8-0
48522 is bringing a trainload of full mineral
wagons along the Liverpool line onto the up
main line. It will pass in front of the 36-lever
signalbox, the signalman having pulled lever
No 6, which lowered the signal by the entrance
to the goods shed, so giving the train the right
to proceed. On the left is the generous
accommodation in the goods yard to compete
with anything that any other railway company
could muster in the town, complete with a
crane that could lift 10 tons. Two lorries are
engaged in picking up sacks of coal from the
wagons for delivery to homes. *(T Lewis)*

Cheadle Heath, 1952. Looking north from
Edgeley Road bridge, this view gives an
insight into the MR's thinking. Across the
rear is the LNWR line from Edgeley Junction
to Northenden Junction, and while the MR had
its up and down tracks through the left-hand
span, the other arch was built to cater for
possible future expansion. In practice, the
right-hand line accessed the building, whose
roof we can see (Oil Well Engineering Co)
east of Hall Lane. Bringing a loaded coal train
towards the station is ex-LNWR 0-8-0 49451.
On the right are some carriage sidings, as
many trains from Manchester terminated at, or
started from, here. A wooden walkway, to
enable carriage cleaning crew access to their
work, is visible. *(ER Morten)*

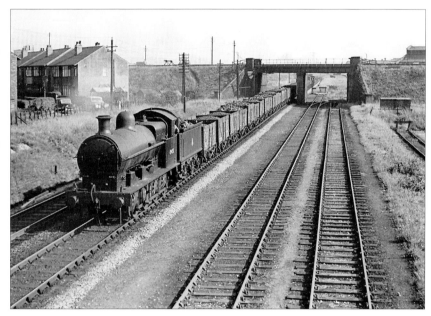

Adswood, 1948. A mile or so after leaving
Cheadle Heath, the MR line passes under the
main LNWR line from Stockport to Crewe. A
set of blind-ended sidings south of Edgeley
Junctions was used to sort wagons for the
Stockport area (top left of picture). On the up
main is an unidentified engine with a train of
empty mineral wagons, and on the down line,
Stanier 2-8-0 48675, still with its former
owners initials on its tender, heads towards
Cheadle Heath with crushed limestone in
hopper wagons. Confident of further
expansion, the company bought enough land
to quadruple the lines at some date, hence the
lines passing through just one side of the
footbridge. During the rebuilding of London
Road as Piccadilly from 1958 to 1966, the MR
line became the main route for London
services. Underpowered Jubilees, and later,
Peak class diesel-electric locomotives, bore
the brunt of heavier trains, a longer route and a
steeper graded line, much of it at 1 in 90 up to
Peak Forest summit, which was higher than
Shap. *(BPC)*

Hazel Grove, 1951. Having just left the depths of Disley tunnel, this excursion from Nottingham is passing Hazel Grove's distant signal. The crew of MR Compound 4-4-0 40929 will need to keep an eye on its speed as it descends the 1 in 200 gradient towards Cheadle Heath; it will need to go no faster than 20mph to gain access to the Glazebrook to Godley line. A sprint to Hunts Cross, and then north to Aintree, will enable punters to attend the Spring Meeting. *(T Lewis)*

Disley Tunnel East Portal. This 2m 346yd tunnel was opened in 1902 – note the cabins for track crews at both ends and a trackside board proclaiming it to be 3,866 yards long. An unidentified 0-6-0 engine is emerging from the east end (stone, with MR emblem) with Disley ahead. Immediately, it will pass over a catch point that would derail it in the event of a runaway. The gradient is 1 in 132 up, with the track being approximately the height of a house higher than when they went in at the eastern end. *(D Ibbotson)*

Disley Tunnel West Portal, 1948. Up above the west end (brick, with date), is the joint line from Marple (Rose Hill) to Macclesfield with a Manchester-bound train being hauled by LNER class C13 4-4-2 7427. Note the drainage ditches in the banks, and the demonstration of the benefits of articulated coaches as space savers. *(D Ibbotson)*

GOWHOL

Derby

UP

New Mills South Junction, 1952. Steaming along the "new" main line, now the up fast, is a train of hopper wagons. Having arrived at Skelton Junction, this train would have turned south at Cheadle Junction and passed through Disley tunnel to arrive here. Ahead is a climb to Peak Forest for a refill of limestone. Stanier 8F 2-8-0 48717 has just passed the 55-lever wooden signalbox, which is still in operation. The original line to Marple, Romiley and Bredbury Junction is on the right – note the

opportunities for transfers between this and the "new" line. *(ER Morten)*

Gowhole Sidings. Established in 1903, was a yard that allowed trains to be marshalled for Manchester or Liverpool via New Mills South Junction. This was similar to the LNER yard at Mottram, which performed a similar function for trains from the east, although it served both up and down lines. Accessed from the slow lines only was a set of sorting sidings. For the up lines there were 10 blind-ended sidings used to assemble trains for Sheffield or Derby, whose lines separated approximately three miles east on the other side of Chinley station. The down lines had a series of 12 loops, complete with an engine release line, where trains for Liverpool, the MR depots at Ancoats and Ashton Road, and connections to the L&Y along the Ardwick Branch, were organised. With no servicing facilities other than a 60ft turntable and water columns, refuelling had to be done at Belle Vue or at Heaton Mersey, necessitating a lot of light engine workings. The system often became congested, resulting in some drivers arriving at a lie-by at the start of their shift and signing off at the end with the train having not moved at all! Coal production doubled between 1855 and 1875 and again by 1913, so from 1907, the MR instituted a system of controlling its freight operations, and had an office near to the western end of the down sidings. *(Signalling Record Society)*

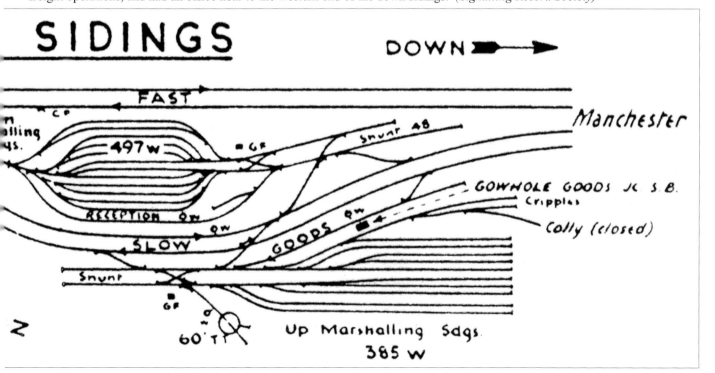

Gowhole, 1947. The fact that the ground wasn't flat was exploited for sorting of wagons at Gowhole. Coal trains destined for Lancashire were heavy, so they would be divided at Rowsley. The gradients on the 14 miles from there to Peak Forest needed 20-ton brake vans and a banking engine, so a down 8F arriving at Rowsley with 70 loaded wagons was split into 2 or 3 trains to be hauled by 4F 0-6-0s and re-assembled here. In the down yard, MR 0-6-0 3723 pulls wagons into the long shunting neck (the "Baltic End") to be "cut" and pushed down to form trains in the loops. To proceed west, an engine was attached to the other end to depart from the loops onto the down slow line. Local destinations of the 76 down departures included Heaton Mersey (7), Ancoats, Ashton Road and Belle Vue (7), with connections to the L&Y (8) and Trafford Park (4) and Portwood. Further afield, destinations included Halewood and Walton in Liverpool and Port Sunlight. In the up yard, a "Crab" has pulled a line of wagons onto one of the shunting lines. After a little push, the wagons will run down the gradient into the sorting lines, depending upon the formation of the train and its destination. The complete train will then be hauled up the gradient onto the up slow line in readiness for its trip over the Pennines. *(JD Darby)*

Buxworth, 1953. As New Mills South Junction was to Gowhole yard in the west, so Buxworth Junction was, to the east. This allowed interchange between the fast and slow lines, making the yard accessible to all trains, in both directions. This train, hauled by an unidentified Stanier 8F 2-8-0, is probably destined for the down sidings at Gowhole. It has just passed the distant signals for the down slow line from Chinley. Notice how the slow lines don't have passenger provision. *(ER Morten)*

Lettuce Train, 1959. Despite this train being from the region covered by this book and running every weekday in season, this is the only photograph I've ever been able to find of it. The market garden area around Broadheath was, and still is, an important part of Cheshire for growing vegetables. Every afternoon, around 3.15 to 4.00pm, a train of specially cleaned out cattle wagons set off from Risley Moss sidings for

London's Somers Town depot. The route would be from Skelton Junction to Cheadle along our chosen Cheshire Lines Railway. Often the load was up to 12 wagons, such was the demand for fresh vegetables in the capital. Later in the season, celery was carried as well. LMS 0-6-0 engine 44236 has just left Chinley on 27th June. *(AC Gilbert)*

Back on the Glazebrook to Godley line from Cheadle Junction

Cheadle Heath, 1951. Passing under the Midland Railway to Cheadle Heath station and beyond is a westbound fitted freight train. Hauling it is one of the powerful LNER K3 class 2-6-0s, 61925 of shed 40A, Lincoln. On the left is the Liverpool curve descending to join in the distance, and on the right, obscured by the engine is a massive set of signals *(below)* that were replaced the following year. *(T Lewis and GH Platt)*

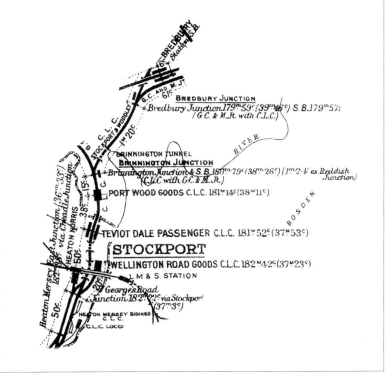

Heaton Mersey West, 1968. Looking west from the ex-MR bridge, we see Stanier 8F 48267 passing the entrance to the engine shed. The controlling signalbox is a typical Cheshire Lines structure, being one of around 50 such buildings that the company built in the 1889-1906 period with a hipped roof and vertical wooden panelling; they originated from their Warrington workshops. For the next ¾ mile east to Georges Road, the main lines were quadruple. The train is passing along the down fast line at the point where the slow and fast lines merge. The line on the extreme left is an up goods loop. Visible in the rear, to the right, is part of the coaling stage for the adjacent loco depot. *(BPC)*

Heaton Mersey West, 1954. The mills and chimneys on the banks of the River Mersey in the background provide a reminder of Stockport's industrial heritage. The sidings in the distance look well used. Obscuring the engine shed is the signalbox, but the signal controlling the exit is visible. The junction controlled by the box is of the fast and slow lines, as only a pair pass west across the River Mersey. Heading for the bridge is LNER class J39 0-6-0 64748. By the tall signal post is a water column for down trains to replenish their tanks. To the left are the up main and up goods loop, while to the right of the train is a pair of up goods lines for fast and slow trains. Curving away in the middle of the picture is a pair of down goods lines for fast and slow trains. This serves to illustrate the amount of traffic that passed along this line. *(Ray Hinton)*

Heaton Mersey West, 1968. Taking on water on the down main line is Stanier 8F 2-8-0 48252. The two notices in the foreground indicate that there are catch points to derail any runaway wagons and prevent them fouling the running lines. One problem with goods in transit is that they are liable to pilfering, and as with all railway companies, the Cheshire Lines had its own police force. By the turn of the century it consisted of a superintendent based at Liverpool Central, an inspector, two detectives and 37 constables. This

was an increase in manpower of 25% over the previous sixteen years, suggesting a growing problem of pilfering of laden wagons in sidings. I suspect that most of their concerns were at the docks in Liverpool. *(FA Wycherley)*

Heaton Mersey West 1960. Looking more like the starting grid for a Formula 1 race than a set of sorting sidings, these three engines are viewed from the lines to the engine shed. Waiting on the down main line to the left, is "Crab" 2-6-0 42854 with a trainload of iron wire, possibly for a factory in Warrington. On the right are two goods lines with LNER class O4 2-8-0 63641 on the fast line, the line to its right being the down slow goods. The middle engine, Stanier 8F 48191, is sitting on the up slow goods line, and could well be involved in shunting in the up sidings that make up the background. The twelve blind-ended sidings that constitute that group had a capacity of 588 wagons. As this is over 150 more than the down sidings, it reflects the levels of activity of the up trains, compared to the down trains. *(Gordon Coltas Trust)*

Heaton Mersey Shed, c.1935. Before 1889, Cheshire Lines engines were catered for in the increasingly cramped two-road shed next to the passenger station at Tiviot Dale. Of the eight roads here, the MR used the southern lines to the right (coding it 21D), while the Cheshire Lines used the remainder (coding it STP). This split style of operation was repeated at Trafford Park several years later. On the MR's lines are 0-6-0 5847 and 4-4-0 5851. Note the intact roof and the smoke cowls above each running line. *(BPC)*

Heaton Mersey Shed, 1960. Twenty five years and a World War later, the shed looks in remarkably good condition, and closure wasn't for another eight years. The entrance to the shed was from a spur almost under the MR girder bridge and in the River Mersey. A turntable close to the coaling stage was resited and enlarged to 70ft in 1952. Above the shed can be seen the water tank that supplied the numerous columns – one is on the right. Illustrating the almost symmetrical nature of the operations here are the different railway company offices, LMS to the right and LNER to the left. The vacant land in front of us was occupied by a coal stack. This arrived in mineral wagons and was shovelled into heaps for use in emergencies. Several Stanier 8F 2-8-0s are in sight as well as LMS 0-6-0s. *(BKB Green)*

Heaton Mersey Shed, 1965. Turning and looking away from the shed, this view shows similar motive power. On the left is Stanier 8F 2-8-0 48515 with sister engine 48329 on the right. In the sandwich is another of Stanier's designs – a 2-6-0, which was his first when appointed CME at the LMS in 1932 (42960 is seen here). It has always been a mystery why he produced such a design, as the company already had over 200 2-6-0s of the "Crab" design, and if they needed any more such engines, it would have been cheaper to have made more of them rather than this small run of 40 engines to a new design. *(Gordon Coltas Trust)*

Heaton Mersey Shed, 1968. An important part of any motive power depot was the refuelling of engines. It is surprising that mechanical means were only developed at some, when there were savings to be made by modest investment of capital at many more. The coaling stage at Heaton Mersey was a large affair, with two tracks leading inside the shed, and it was possible to service engines on both sides. Inside, the coal was shovelled from wagons into tubs, which were then pushed out of the

building along the guide rails, above the engine, and tipped into the tender waiting below. To fill such a space took many 10-cwt tubs and quite a time – and there was always another engine waiting behind! The 1952 rebuilding of the facilities seems to have missed this important side of things. Two months before closure we see Stanier 8F 2-8-0 No 48252 getting ready to be refuelled. The trophy hunters have already stolen the shed plate, so the number has been painted on. It closed on 6th May 1968 as code 9F, which it had been for most of its 20-odd years with BR apart from brief periods as 19D, 13C and 17E. *(BPC)*

Heaton Mersey Shed, 1934. It is rather rare to see pictures of engines receiving attention at the shear-legs as they weren't often used; there were actually two sets here! Continuing the theme of separate yet together, both the LNER and LMS sides of the shed had their own set. Utilizing the latter company's "legs" is 4F 0-6-0 4286. By hooking under the footplate, the whole engine could be lifted up and

here, the rear wheels have been removed for attention. There was only ever one turntable though. On the left is one of the "Flatiron" 0-6-4Ts (2008) that hauled commuter trains to Heaton Mersey station. *(Kidderminster Railway Museum)*

Heaton Mersey East Junction, 1968. Taking water on the up goods loop before it proceeds east, is Stanier 2-8-0 8F 48115, on 9th April. It will be able to proceed when the signalman pulls lever No 65 to lift the single arm to the off position, as well as those moving the facing point lock and the point onto the main line. Just behind the train was the connection from Heaton Mersey station. The age-old tradition of sheeting loads and tying them down still persisted even though BR was relieved of its obligation to be a common carrier by the 1962 Transport Act. *(BPC)*

Heaton Mersey East Junction, 1960. To cope with the establishment of industries in the area, and the sorting of wagons, the Cheshire Lines built up and down sets of sidings at Heaton Mersey. In the background is the Didsbury Road overbridge with the chocolate factory on the left; the main lines are in front of it. Just visible before the lines sweep under the bridge is the ground frame for the sidings in the factory. Although the sidings are becoming overgrown, the signals show up well. All appear to be of Cheshire Lines origin and of lower-quadrant type. Wooden posts, cute finials and ornate ironwork were the order of the day. A company water column was available for engines to refill their tanks without having to make the trip to Heaton Mersey shed. *(G Harrop)*

Heaton Mersey East Junction, before 1969. Controlling events here was a box on the up side from the early 1880s, when the MR arrived via the South District Railway, only to be replaced in 1896 by a box that was itself replaced in 1935. On the other side of the main lines was Heaton Mersey Sidings signalbox, which lasted until 1934 when its functions were transferred to this box. The 68-lever box was in the tradition of the Cheshire Lines with the nameplate fixed to the western end. So busy was the freight through this area that there were four goods lines in addition to the two main lines. Trains had to obey a 20mph speed restriction when using this junction. *(RK Blencowe)*

Georges Road, 1954. To proceed east, the original railway company, the Stockport, Timperley & Altrincham Railway, had to pass under the LNWR viaduct carrying the line from Stockport Edgeley to Manchester London Road. As the line east of this viaduct was lower down in the River Mersey valley, it would have to be at quite a steep gradient, and the company also decided to cover over the descending line so as to be able to use the

land above it. Coming up the 1 in 72 gradient emerging from the 246-yard tunnel, having left Tiviot Dale station a few minutes earlier, is the 5.05pm from Rotherham (Westgate) to Manchester Central. There was no return working. *(CHA Townley)*

Georges Road Goods Yard, 1967. This was a very important Cheshire Lines railhead on the north side of the Mersey in Stockport, and not only was it a junction of the main lines, but three sets of sidings also met there. Coming towards us on its way east with a load of empty coal wagons is Standard class 9F 2-10-0 92106 on 1st June. It is passing along the fast line, and will soon descend down the gradient into a short tunnel under the LNWR viaduct and on to Tiviot Dale station. In 1884, when the route was widened with additional lines to the south, they were carried over Georges Road by a plate girder bridge with additional strengthening. The bracket signal, obscuring the signalbox, is a wonderful example of the variety of semaphore signals that could exist. The large arm is to control the passage of trains over the junction, and under it is a calling-on arm that allowed trains to pass the signal (when it was on) dead-slow as far as the next signal. This allowed one engine to come up

behind another already occupying the section. While commonly used in terminal roads to allow the release of trapped engines, it also was useful to let trains on gradients clear them before stopping, so that a blockage of the line didn't occur (or worse, a train rolling backwards down the 1 in 69). The left-hand arm had replaced two larger arms some time previously, and indicated access to the through lines. Shunting in Georges Road sidings is class 5 4-6-0 45269. It is hard to believe that behind the photographer electric trains had been running to Crewe for seven years. *(Gordon Coltas Trust)*

Georges Road, c.1967. Looking west from the steps of the signalbox, we see a train of vans on the up fast lines. Class 5 4-6-0 45190 has lost its shed plate – most likely stolen by a souvenir hunter. The train is crossing Georges Road with the original brick parapet on the right and the steelwork for the extension on the left. Shunting in the coal yard behind us and in the Club House sidings over the bridge, would be carried out along the connecting line immediately in front of us. The three arms on the signal post indicate the route an engine is to take, and the wooden boards allow men to walk across the bridge without tripping over the operating wires. *(Steam Image)*

Georges Road Junction, 1974. When the 50-lever frame was stolen in 1981, the box had only been closed a few months, having lasted from 1884. It has a large overhanging roof with ornamental roof brackets, and a porch roof sloping at the same angle as the main roof – typical of others in the first Cheshire Lines standard style, and dating it to between 1884 and 1889. The all-brick construction was a departure though, as was the position of the nameboard. *(Inset)* Next to the signalbox, and photographed in 1978, was this original post that showed the gradients down and under Wellington Road (1 in 72) and the line west (1 in 400). *(Both, A Sommerfield)*

Opposite page top: **Georges Road Coal Yard Stables, 1966.** In the coal yard here there were six pairs of sidings widely spaced out so that horses could reverse their carts. These animals needed care and attention, as well as somewhere to be housed overnight, and fields were in short supply! This building was therefore built for stabling horses, with bales of hay and straw often being stored in the roof – note the accesses on the gable ends. These heavy horses were probably Suffolk Punch and Clydesdale breeds, each animal weighing in at around a ton. Things changed as a result of the wars, however, and the 1948 outbreak of equine flu resulted in most being replaced by the mid 1950s by Scammell 3-wheel "mechanical horses" with trailers.

Opposite page bottom: **Georges Road Coal Yard Deliveries, 1966.** By this time, rail deliveries had ceased, and lorry loads were tipped at various places in the yard, such as here against the wall at the bottom of the viaduct. For generations, up until the mid-1960s, almost every home, factory and office had deliveries from coal merchants, and Robert Tonge was one who operated from the yard. Men are shovelling coal into sacks (weighed using the device at the end of the lorry) containing 1/20 of a ton. This was known as a hundredweight (cwt) even though it weighed 112 pounds! On arrival at a house, they would pick up one sac from the back of the lorry, carry it to where it was needed, and tip out the contents – not surprisingly, coal dirt became ingrained in the men's skin. The weekly delivery of bags of coal, the storage of it, and the clearing of the ashes and smoke, have all but faded from the town's scene. North Sea Gas, central heating and the Clean Air Act have made this business a shadow of its former self.

Wellington Road Goods Shed, early 1960s. As in Leeds, and many other towns in the country, a road named after the victor at Waterloo became a centre for rail activity. In Stockport, there were two large warehouses on this road. To the north was the LNWR building in Heaton Norris, and to the east of the road was the Cheshire Lines building next to the viaduct. Access was from loops with a capacity for 122 wagons on the down side of the main lines, and controlled by Georges Road Junction signalbox. Lines from them passed through the arches into the shed behind it (on the left) and there were two sidings to the right of the weighbridge. Carts would back up under the canopy of the shed to be loaded. We are standing by the vehicle entrance to the yard, with the Glazebrook to Godley line several feet beneath us. *(All, Stockport Libraries)*

Stewart Street, 1963. Between Georges Road yard and Tiviot Dale station were three tunnels. From the west was Wellington Road (under the viaduct and the goods depot), then Brownsword (under Wilkinson Road), and then Tiviot Dale tunnel (under Lancashire Hill). Between the tunnels were sheer-sided cuttings in the sandstone rock. Looking west towards Georges Road *(above)* this view shows a train emerging from the short, 39-yard, Brownsword tunnel. Heading east is Stanier 2-8-0 48118 with a train of empty mineral wagons. As the gradient is against trains heading west, there is a trap point on the down line to derail any breakaways, and prevent them crashing into following trains. On the night of 23rd/24th March 1936 such an accident happened. A west-bound coal train had stopped at the signals, and on restarting, a coupling broke leaving the rear 30 wagons to head into the tunnel. The subsequent derailment of wagons, and the spillage of coal, blocked the line completely. Gangs worked through the night to open one line around 7am. Turning round to face the east *(opposite page top)* this view shows the line curving round the corner before it plunges into Tiviot Dale tunnel. Immediately in front of us is a signal with a sighting board for down trains. Trains heading west towards Georges Road would obey the bracket signal which is cantilevered out from the side of the cutting to aid sighting. The lesser-used route, whose signal is on the lower post, is for trains to transfer to the down goods as soon as they emerge from the tunnel. *(Both, Kidderminster Railway Museum)*

Opposite page: **Brownsword Tunnel, March 1968.** Once there was a footpath from Love Lane, along Wilkinson Road, across the recreation ground. and over the line by Brownsword's works to link up with Stewart Street. Some of the Glazebrook to Godley line was under Wilkinson Road where it went into a short tunnel. Due to the passage of time and the ravages of countless exhausts, the brick lining of the tunnel deteriorated to such an extent that it had to be renewed or removed; this picture shows how the latter was done. The sequence involved removal of material above the tunnel to expose the brick skin, and the laying of timber baulks (often sleepers) over the track. As can be seen, this had to be done with all the materials being unloaded from a train in attendance. Explosive charges were laid in the brickwork, and subsequently the tunnel roof ended up lying on the timbers. Man power, aided by machinery, loaded the rubble into wagons and the line could be reopened. Special care was needed to ensure that the signalling apparatus (such as the wire on the left) wasn't damaged. Stewart Street was eventually removed to make room for the M63 motorway. *(G Harrop)*

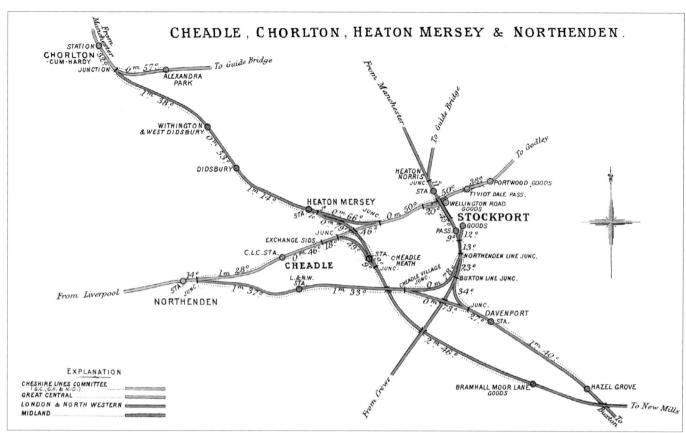

CHEADLE, CHORLTON, HEATON MERSEY & NORTHENDEN.

Stockport, Tiviot Dale Station, 1905. On 1st December 1865, the Stockport, Timperley & Altrincham Railway opened this station on Tiviot Dale as part of the line east from Portwood to Deansgate Junction near Altrincham. As the Portwood and Woodley Railway had been operating for almost two years, a through line existed, skirting Manchester to the south. It offered passengers a route to London, Liverpool and Yorkshire, without having to travel to Manchester first. Whether or not it was meant to resemble a set of cloisters, the 32 arches were a novel way to support a canopy. *(J Ryan Collection)*

Tiviot Dale, around 1902. While the nameboard proudly displays the station's name, those with an eye for accuracy will note that the station is actually in Lancashire! The county boundary (the River Mersey) passes just behind our backs, and crosses under the line beyond the eastern end of the station, which is therefore north-east of the river. Murray's *Handbook for Cheshire* (1879) described the station here as, "A pretty brick building with an open arcade in front". An important train, probably from London, is expected judging by the number of waiting cabs. Notice the different sizes, some for one or two people (a Hansom cab, or more correctly a Chapman cab) and others for larger parties (a Growler). The station forecourt was guarded jealously by the railway company, and while it allowed any cab to drop passengers off to catch trains, it allowed only certain cabs ("privileged" ones) to wait on their land to pick up passengers. Cab operators had to pay for this privilege. Whilst cabs had been licensed for over fifty years (including a knowledge test) in the capital, it took until 1896 for the introduction of the first driving test for its horse cabmen. The small structure on the left may well have been a shelter for the cabmen to await their fares. *(Stockport Libraries)*

Tiviot Dale, 1908. Tiviot Dale station would be thought of as well-sited today, being close to the main business and shopping centre of the town. This is probably why a royal party used this station rather than its larger neighbour at Edgeley. The party arrived in the town shortly after 3pm on 7th July on a train that originated in Chester. After the Prince of Wales had inspected the guard-of-honour, the party, including the Princess, was driven to the town hall, where due ceremony was given to the opening of the building (the foundation stone having been laid in 1904) and then the group caught a train back to Chester at 4.40pm. The nameboard is fascinating, as all three railway companies that made up the managing committee have their names written out, with some of the destinations underneath. *(J Ryan Collection)*

Tiviot Dale Station, 1967. The large station forecourt inevitably became a car park. Viewed as classic cars today are a Mini van, a Morris Minor, a Ford Anglia 105E, an Austin A30 and a VW "Beetle". The site chosen to build this station was sandwiched between a crossing of the River Mersey in the east and an outcrop of sandstone to the west. Cramped conditions were featured in one of Engels's observations about Stockport, albeit some twenty-five years before the line opened. He remarked, "Stockport is renowned throughout the entire district as one of the duskiest, smokiest holes, and looks, indeed, especially when viewed

from the viaduct, excessively repellent. But far more repulsive are the cottages and cellar dwellings for the working class, which stretch in long rows through all parts of the town from the valley bottoms to the crest of the hill," The station and the adjacent chapel were knocked down to make way for the M63 (now the M60). *(Stations UK)*

Tiviot Dale Station, around 1962. So that trains at the platforms wouldn't block the movement of other trains through the station, two loops were constructed off the main lines to serve the platforms. This view is looking west with the lines disappearing into a short, 225-yard, tunnel, with buildings on Lancashire Hill above. With the main buildings on the down, left-hand side, access to the up side was effected by this curved covered footbridge. On the down platform was a waiting room and a refreshment room, with toilets at the far end. On the up platform were waiting rooms and toilets. Behind us were bays in both platforms, the two on the down side having roofs over them until the early 1950s. *(RK Blencowe Negative Archive)*

Tiviot Dale Station, 1966. The provision for the two passengers seems more than adequate to protect them from the rain. I have yet to see a picture with the gable ends of the roof filled in. On the platform are the inevitable parcels trolleys and three benches. The lady isn't making use of the waiting rooms, despite the date (December), but the man might have had use of the toilet at the far end. Lurking to the right is one of the banking engines that pushed freight trains to Woodley. From 1875, there was a service from here to London Road via Reddish. The opening of the Manchester South District line five years later reduced the frequency of this service, which disappeared completely during the Great War. Management of the refreshment rooms was by the firm of Spiers & Pond, but from 1st October 1906,

the GNR took over this function here and at other CLR stations such as Warrington and Southport. *(A Sommerfield)*

Tiviot Dale, mid-1960s. At the opening it was recognized that Stockport would be a terminal station for many services, so some engine maintenance facilities would be needed. Consequently, a turntable and a short two-road shed with room for six tender engines were provided to the north of the platforms. In 1886, 22 engines were working from the shed, making it very cramped when, as on Sundays, services were at their least. After the opening of Heaton Mersey shed in 1889, however, it was relegated to being a watering place for banking engines. Viewed after closure, this view shows a small compact yard, where the through lines provided opportunities for engines to run round their coaches. Hidden by the building in front of us was a side exit from the station directly onto Lancashire Hill, to the right-hand side of the recently-demolished (in 1966) Hanover Chapel. *(G Harrop)*

Tiviot Dale, 1963. Having set off from Liverpool Central station some two hours ago, Stanier 2-6-4T 42598 has arrived after providing a service to all stations, including Widnes, along the way. Notice the magnificent facing signal gantry. The left-hand arm controlled the bay platform, which was chiefly used by banking engines. The through lines were controlled by the other two arms, the shorter post being for the platform line, and the blackened post being a reminder of the sheer volume of passing steam trains. *(Peter Fitton)*

Tiviot Dale, 1963. Passing through with empty coal wagons on the up main line is LNER O4 class 2-8-0 63575 on 20th November. Smoke often used to cloak the platforms after the passing of such trains in colder weather due to the presence of the River Mersey and the short tunnel the train has just emerged from. The use of such small wagons reflects the continual battle waged between the colliery owners and the carriers: the railways. The latter wanted larger wagons to reduce maintenance costs, but the former would not go to the expense of altering the loading machinery at the pithead. The empties are from Bidston, on the Wirral, to Wath marshalling yard in the heart of the South Yorkshire coalfield. *(Peter Fitton)*

Banking Engine at Tiviot Dale, 1965. Woodley, to the east, was the highest point along the line, and approaching it were some the longest and steepest gradients on the Cheshire Lines. To push the trains (albeit frequently empty wagons) up the slope, banking engines were extensively used. These were often from Heaton Mersey shed (9F in later BR days) and they would wait in Tiviot Dale Station, either in the platform or bay roads. They would buffer-up to the rear of passing goods trains, and would crossover to the down line at Woodley to go back to Tiviot Dale station to await the next train. Nearing

the end of its useful life on such a trip is Stanier 2-6-0 42960 on 15th September. In the years up to the 1950s, this job was performed by an N5 0-6-2T. As the Cheshire Lines was a joint undertaking, it passed bills to its constituent owners for their agreed share of the cost to run the line. The 1901 bill presented to the joint company by the GCR showed that approximately a quarter of the costs for banking and pilot engines was produced by this short (nearly 3-mile section). *(Gordon Coltas Trust)*

Portwood Viaduct, 1968. The signalbox was taken out of use in July 1967, and all pointwork was either removed or bolted to allow passage along the main lines only. This was the route that Stanier 8F 2-8-0 48765 will be taking coming down the gradient from Woodley with its trainload of coal. The line was on a series of 18 bridges all the way from Portwood, so to call it a viaduct, is being a touch generous. In the late 1950s, the BR upper-quadrant bracket signal replaced a post with two lower-quadrant arms that was located on the other side of the line. *(BPC)*

Tiviot Dale, 1957. Not far from its home shed at Heaton Mersey, is ex-MR 0-6-0 44261 with a down freight on 1st June. The down signals are fascinating. On the side of the viaduct is a two-armed bracket for the platform or the down loop. On the other side of the twisting line, is a post with two arms on it. This probably controls the crossover and the entry to the two down sidings to the right, leading to a down bay and a carriage siding. *(Ray Hinton)*

Tiviot Dale, 1962. At the eastern end of the station, the lines were carried on a large girder bridge over the confluence of the rivers Tame and Mersey. Passing over the rivers is the 10.44am from Mottram Yard to Shotwick coal train. Showing a through mineral train headcode is LNER class O4 2-8-0 63598 on 9th April. The rear wagons are going underneath an interesting signal gantry, replacing the signalling arrangements in the above picture. The signalman in the next box will have pulled lever no 5 to raise the second arm

from the right, while the arm to the extreme right would be for the platform line. Access to the up side sidings, a crossover and the bays behind us on the down side, were controlled by the other arms on the gantry. In fact, the line we are standing on leads to the bays, while the points the engine is passing over lead to the down platform from the main line. *(G Coltas Trust)*

Opposite: **Portwood, 1960s.** This view is looking up, in both senses of the word, towards Brinnington Junction, just after the line passes over Marsland Street behind us. Around here was the site of Portwood station (1863-75), and it also marks the place where the Stockport & Woodley line finished and the Stockport, Timperley & Altrincham Railway began. On the right is Portwood goods warehouse, while on the left are the coal drops serving a yard accessed at the junction of Brewery and Marsland Streets. Between the main lines and the goods shed are a series of loops. Having descended the gradient, down trains would stop there to have their brakes unpinned. The signal gantry has recently replaced a fine display of Cheshire Lines signals, those for the main line being on the wrong side to aid sighting. The two arms on the right are for the loops, and as Tiviot Dale box has by now closed, the need for a distant arm on the left-hand post has gone. *(Stockport Libraries)*

Tiviot Dale, undated.
When things go wrong on railways, they do so in a big way. Standing on the up main line we see a tank engine being re-railed, having wrecked most of the lines. The crane is lifting one end of the casualty onto the track, and then it will turn its attention to the other end. We are looking towards the station, over the confluence of the Rivers Goyt and Tame that flow westwards to become the Mersey. The distinctive bracket signal will be replaced by one with a different style of support for the cross beam. The street access to the station was actually called Teviotdale on some maps.
(Stockport Libraries)

Opposite page top: **Portwood. 1963.** This section of the line initially climbed at 1 in 111, then at 1 in 92 stiffening to quite a stretch at 1 in 80. Sections of 1 in 150 and 1 in 60 would be encountered before level ground at Woodley junction about three miles away. Consequently, eastbound trains relied on banking engines that waited at the station to assist them. Coming off the viaduct that carries the line east through the Portwood district of Stockport is Hughes-Fowler "Crab" 2-6-0 42792 on a trip freight from Heaton Mersey sidings to Dewsnap sidings.

Opposite page bottom: **Portwood. 1963.** Banking the train seen above on this occasion (13th February) was 3F 0-6-0 44282. On the up side was a coal yard with 3F 0-6-0 44501 shunting there. In the opposite direction trains used an adjacent down loop to let off their brakes. This site was one of approximately 1,000 on the BR network where pinning down, or letting off, of brakes went on, and in its 1955 Modernization Plan, BR estimated that this needed 10,000 man-hours per week, hence the desire to introduce fully-fitted freight trains. These could travel at higher speeds, would need fewer engines, and would save the time previously spent on this kind of activity. However, continuous braking was estimated to cost £75M.

This page top: **Portwood. 1963.** On 15th September banking was provided by Stanier 8F 2-8-0 48666. While the passenger station that opened with the line had a short life (closing in 1875) the goods facilities flourished.
(All, Gordon Coltas Trust)

STOCKPORT, WOODLEY, and GODLEY JUNCTION.—Cheshire Lines.

	Up.	Week Days.																		Sundays.					
Miles		mrn	mrn	mrn	mrn	mrn	mrn	mrn	mrn	aft	aft	aft	aft	aft	aft	aft	aft				mrn	aft	aft	aft	aft	aft
	Tiviot Dale Station, Stockport......dep.	6 14	6 45	8 30	9 7	9 46	1055	1126	1153	1 15	2 22	5 20	6 7	4 69	0 9	55	1020				9 30	2 0	4 45	5 50	8 15	9 15
3	Woodley 664, 665......	6 22	6 52	8 36	9 14	9 54	11 2	1133	12 0	1 22	2 28	5 26	6 33	7 52	9	7 10	3 1027				9 37	2 7	4 52	5 57	8 22	9 22
5¼	Godley Junction......arr.	6 30	....	8 43	....	10 0	....	1141	....	....	2 35	5 33	6 40	....		....	1011				9 43	....	4 59	6 4	....	9 30

GODLEY JUNCTION, WOODLEY, and STOCKPORT.—Cheshire Lines.

	Down.	Week Days.																		Sundays.					
Miles		mrn	mrn	mrn	mrn	mrn	mrn	mrn	aft	aft	aft	aft	aft	aft	aft	aft	aft		aft	aft	mrn	mrn	aft	aft	aft	aft
	Godley Junction......dep.	3b55	....	7 35	....	9 30	....	1055	....	1 29	....	2 12	5 10	6 57	8	....	....		1110	....	3 55	1020	....	7 20	8 15	....	1015
2¼	Woodley............	....	6 19	7 42	8 10	9 37	1034	11 3	12 2	1 19	....	2 23	3 19	5 16	6 12	7 15	8 18	1034	11 5	1116	....	1026	4 7	7 27	8 22	9 0	1022
5	Stockport (Tiviot Dale)arr.	4 5	6 26	7 49	8 17	9 46	1041	1110	1210	1 26	1 50	2 29	3 25	5 22	6 20	7 23	8 25	1041	1112	1123	....	4 5	1032	5 37	3 48	29 9	7 1029

b Except Mondays.

Brinnington Junction, 1954. Looking east we see the rising main line straight ahead, and then curving right for the tunnel. On the left is the 1875 line to Reddish Junction, which ran parallel this line, and eventually curved left; this lasted for 90 years. A passenger service ran from London Road to Tiviot Dale using this Portwood Branch, and it was also useful for goods trains from Ancoats toward Liverpool. It was on the left-hand side of this line that the signalbox was sited until 1881. Then, the loops and sidings were constructed, and a box was put onto the other side, only to be rebuilt in 1895. The hipped roof, vertical cladding and all-wooden construction indicate one of company's own 40-lever boxes. The taller post on the bracket is for the main line, and the middle and right-hand arms are for entry to the loops and the goods warehouse. After a fire in 1975, signalling here was done by the frame from Cock Lane (Guide Bridge) relocated and installed in two garden sheds, but this too suffered at the hand of vandals. The motorway resulted in the demise of the line in the early 1980s.
(Signalling Record Society, Scrimgeour Collection. Map reproduced by kind permission of the Ordnance Survey)

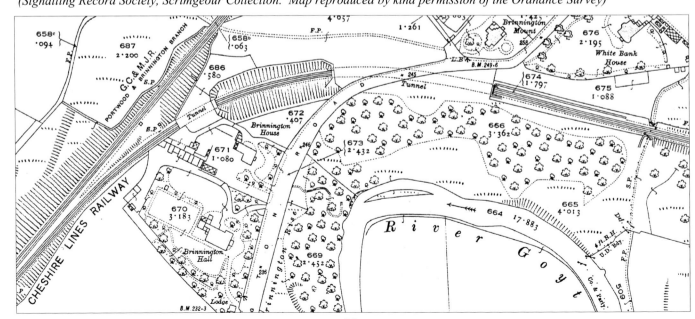

Brinnington Tunnel, 1962. Due to the 1 in 80 gradient here, Standard class 5 73002 is coasting down from tunnel No 2 towards Stockport at almost 7.20pm with the 5.30 from Sheffield Midland to Manchester Central. Contributing to the slow timing for the 45-mile journey were nine minutes of catching up time at Chinley – hardly an inducement to travel by train. The line contained trap points to prevent loose wagons that had broken free from going backwards down the slope on the wrong line. *(Gordon Coltas Trust)*

Brinnington Tunnel. This is the eastern portal of the tunnel. The line here is close to the River Goyt so while the land rises to the right, requiring a retaining wall, it drops away to the left down to the river. It was the massive bend in the river *(see map)*

that dictated where the line was built, and when it opened in 1863, this 168-yard tunnel (No 2) was opened to allow the line to pass under the Brinnington Road just a few feet above. Six chains to the east, the line originally passed through another short, 32-yard tunnel (No 1), but in the summer of 1931, it was converted into a cutting with retaining walls. This involved the removal of the land down to the lining of the tunnel before it could be removed, so on Sunday 12th July at 6am, the occupants of the few nearby houses, Brinnington Hall and House, were awoken by the sounds of explosives. By 9am, the up line had been cleared enough to allow passage of a train for Sheffield. *(D Ibbotson)*

Opposite page top: **Bredbury, 1960.** Just over 1½ miles east of Stockport, the Stockport & Woodley Railway passes under the MS&LR joint line used by the MR for its Romiley to Ashbury services (on the viaduct in the background). In 1875, a short west-to-south curve was put in to link the two lines. At around 3.30pm, "Crab" 2-6-0 42759 has just come down the "Marple Curve" from Romiley, obeying the 25mph speed restriction. It joins the Cheshire Lines at Bredbury Junction (obscured by the bushes) and is heading west. It started its journey five minutes after the St Pancras to Manchester Central express left Derby Midland, and while the latter scurried through the Peak District to "Cottonopolis" in around 100 minutes, this train would stop at 25 stations between the two cities. A 13-minute wait at Miller's Dale allowed for Buxton connections, and although the average speed was only 20mph, it provided a service commensurate with the demands of the time, together with connections to and from some expresses. The tall signals controlled the up lines at the junction – the box is on the left. Both posts have lower repeater arms. *(Peter Hutchinson)*

Opposite page bottom: **Bredbury, 1965.** Passing east is a train of empty mineral wagons hauled by "Crab" 2-6-0 42859 on 9th October. The first signalbox was a little to the east, but that stone cabin was replaced in 1931 by this brick one to house the 21 levers. Bredbury, an ancient settlement mentioned in the 1086 Domesday Book, appears rural, but coal mining, steel works, textiles and brick-making caused the population to increase threefold from the first census in 1801. *(Peter Fitton)*

This page top: **Bredbury Junction, 1965.** Passing east with a trainload of empty coal wagons is Standard class 2-10-0 92158 – note the excessively tall signals with repeater arms. When running east, trains would be going up a gradient of 1 in 80 or more, and after the sinuous twists on the Portwood viaduct, speeds would hardly be very high. The need for such sky-borne signals (one with a repeater arm) is therefore puzzling. Changing the oil in the signal lamps couldn't have been a popular job, especially in winter. *(Peter Fitton)*

Middle: **Bredbury Junction Signal Cabin, 1955.** A wonderful insight into the world of a signalbox, with the Spartan walls and floor, single-glazed windows, and lack of insulation in the roof. It needed a good stove in the winter and evenings. To the left, on the desk, is the log book in which every train that passed was recorded. The footboard enabled a good force to be exerted to pull the point rodding or the wire to the signals. On the shelf are the instruments that show if a section is occupied or not and the bell for communication with adjacent boxes. *(Signalling Record Society, Scrimgeour Collection)*

Right: **Bredbury, 1965.** Stanier 8F 2-8-0 48190 has just pulled its train of coal wagons under the brick arches of the MS&LR/MR joint line from Romiley to Ashburys, while, on the joint line is class 5 4-6-0 44807 with a southbound freight train heading towards Romiley. The small bridge across the line to Timperley Farm, and the Ashton Road beyond, necessitated the tall signals in both directions. *(Peter Fitton)*

Connections via the "Marple Curve"

Bredbury, 1962. The Cheshire Lines offered several connections to other parts of the railway system, hence its strategic importance. However, there was a price to pay. Not only were the connections subject to speed restrictions, but they also had some steep gradients, as exemplified by the 1 in 71 curve from Bredbury Junction to Romiley. Opening for goods on 15th February 1875, and passengers on 1st April, was this just over 1¼-mile link built by two of the partners of the Cheshire Lines, the MS&LR and the MR. Trains from Manchester destined for Sheffield or Derby will have found this curve useful. With the time around 7.20pm, an all-stations train for Derby hauled by 2-6-4T 42306 is working hard up the gradient, having negotiated the junction. The curve comes to lie parallel with the joint line from Ashburys to Romiley, and Bredbury station is up on the embankment, complete with standard MR fencing. *(Gordon Coltas Trust)*

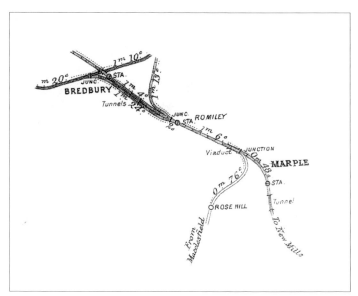

Bredbury Tunnels, 1951. North of Bredbury station is a pair of 160-yard tunnels *(see map)* that the joint lines pass through. Looking south we see the joint line from Ashburys on the right and the curve from the junction on the left. The difference in height between the two sets of lines can be seen to diminish as the curve comes up to meet the joint line. Jubilee class 4-6-0 45696 *Arethusa* heads a Derby-bound train towards Romiley. The signals are new, having just replaced a splendid pair of lower-quadrant arms on wooden posts.
(T Lewis, N Preedy Archive)

Romiley Approach, 1955. Having slowed down to turn from the main line at Bredbury Junction, and climbed up the gradient on the curve, this train must now obey a speed limit to negotiate the junctions ahead. Running from Liverpool to Nottingham, its progress will be slow due to such difficulties. *(ER Morten)*

Romiley, 1933. What a wonderful picture! LNER Sentinel steam railcar 601 is pulling a 6-wheel carriage up the slope towards Romiley bound for Marple; the service is the 1pm from Stockport Tiviot Dale. The train will have arrived here after leaving Bredbury Junction through the tunnel on the left; on the right are the joint lines to Ashburys. The service returned at 2.05pm, and additional 3rd class seating was provided by the 6-wheel coach. This shuttle was repeated at 4.50 (out) and 5.20 (return) sandwiched in between trips to Liverpool and back. When first built, this unit was based at Stockport, and worked to Godley, Hyde, Altrincham, New Mills and Northwich. Later, it was shedded at Brunswick. *(RD Pollard)*

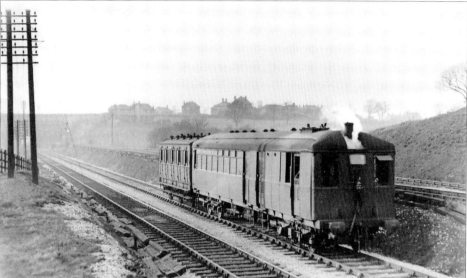

Romiley Departure, c.1966. Of course, down trains didn't have it all plain sailing – it will take the skill of the footplate crew to ensure that this Sheffield to Manchester Central train stays within the speed limits. Class 5 4-6-0 44708 has just left Romiley station and is passing along the curve towards Bredbury junction. This picture encapsulates the attempts by the Midland Railway to reach Manchester. Initially it used the Woodley line (on the left) and then it had a hand in building the joint line to reach Manchester London Road (the middle pair of lines). Having been given notice to quit that terminus, and with the construction of Central station, it then used the Cheshire Lines (the right-hand pair). Frustrated by all these attempts to be competitive, it finally built the Disley cut-off via Cheadle Heath. *(J Fairclough)*

Connections Along the Joint Lines to Romiley

The Midland Railway in the East of Manchester

The reasons why the Midland Railway came to own a magnificent passenger terminus station on one side of Manchester and a vast goods depot on the other side of the city have their origins in the 1850s. In an attempt to penetrate the Manchester stronghold of the LNWR without the expense of its own station, the MR was party to several lines from the original MS&LR line from Hyde to Marple from 1862. In this way the Midland's passenger trains gained access to London Road station. The company also built an extensive goods depot to the north of the approaches at Ancoats, opening on 2nd May 1870. The MR and the MS&LR were joint builders of a shorter link to Manchester from Romiley than the original MS&LR route around the contours via Guide Bridge (opening on 17th May 1875), but so congested was London Road station becoming that the LNWR, gave the MR notice to quit within the following three years. The development of Central station then isolated the older Ancoats goods station. Access could be gained from MR metals from New Mills South Junction and the Cheshire Lines via Brinnington Junction, but while London Road passenger station and Ancoats goods station were physically so close, their fortunes are now worlds apart. Piccadilly is probably the busiest passenger station outside London – a mantle that Victoria once held, but Ancoats is now a business park, and the approaches are an environmental corridor along the banks of the River Medlock.

Ancoats Goods Depot, 1960s. As well as the connection to the L&Y system, the almost 1-mile long MR Ancoats branch of 1870 pierced right into the heart of the city with an extensive 70-acre depot at Ancoats, costing £½ million. This view is from Ancoats Hall, which was then a BR Recreation Club. Weaving its way below us is Great Ancoats Street, with the sidings and a shed-full of wagons behind. St Andrew's church is in the background, and a trolleybus is emerging under the wire from Every Street on the right. Along the main road are hoardings advertising everything from margarine to stout. Just out of sight, the main road is crossed by a line from the goods depot to a grain store – the tall building on the right.
(Manchester Library & Information Service)

Access to Ancoats Goods Depot, 1960s.
After leaving the MS&LR line at Ashburys West Junction, the Ancoats branch threw off the curve to the L&Y line at Ancoats Junction, becoming quadruple to the extensive sheds at Ancoats. This branch passed under the L&Y Ardwick branch from Ardwick to Park, and then under Ashton Old Road, where the steelwork is still *in situ* opposite Lime Bank Street. The line then climbed up over the River Medlock, Palmerston Road and Pin Mill Brow before entering the goods depot. While the purpose of the picture was to record for posterity the printing works at the junction of the last two named roads (removed as part of a slum-clearance programme) it has some value to our account. Passing behind the structure is the elevated line and (fortunately for us) an engine is waiting, probably to take a train from the goods depot. A fraction more to the right we would have seen the controlling signalbox at Palmerston Road. Note the wires for the environmentally-friendly trolleybuses suspended from the street light columns.
(Manchester Library & Information Service)

Ashton Road, c.1960. Next to the Ancoats goods depot is the large MR-built coal and cattle station at Ashton Road. To allow access to the four running lines in front was this 20-lever wooden signalbox. Behind, and at a slightly lower level, are the GCR sidings of Ardwick goods yard with an unidentified 0-6-0 performing shunting duties. Behind that are some carriage sidings with the main GCR electrified line to Sheffield beyond. There was extensive damage caused by German bombing in World War II, and greater accuracy could have brought activities to a halt. *(G Harrop)*

Reddish Junction, 1953. Having just passed over the viaduct that spans the River Tame, an RCTS special train takes the Brinnington line. After 1½ miles, ex-L&Y 2-4-2T 50644 will meet Cheshire Lines metals. Controlling events is this small 17-lever signalbox, to the rear of which passes the joint line to Romiley, which now has a new station called Brinnington. This opened on 12th December 1977, just north of the site of Lingard's Lane Colliery. *(CHA Townley)*

Bredbury Station, 1958. Like so many cities, the introduction of DMUs transformed train services. Here is a 2-car unit at the up platform with a service from Manchester. The 20-lever signalbox is interesting – being on the embankment, it is made of wood and is of MR style. It is too far away from the Redhouse Lane bridge, and too low to afford a good view over it, and it is on the wrong side of the tracks to be sighted by trains coming round the curve. Note the tall Cheshire Lines post on the lower level lines, complete with repeater arm, its height allowing it to be seen well before the bridge, as trains will be going downhill here. *(RB Priestley)*

Bredbury Tunnels, 1933.
Having passed through the 160-yard tunnel, the line from Bredbury station is parallel to the line from Bredbury Junction, but at a higher level. Both lines are on an up gradient – the former at 1 in 94 and the latter at 1 in 71. The railway companies thought it would be cheaper to tunnel through, rather than create a deep cutting. Typical motive power along these lines, "Crab" 2-6-0 13124, heads excursion no 740 – probably from Belle Vue to the East Midlands. This engine was one of a batch of five that the LMS experimented with a couple of years earlier. This involved adding Lentz RC poppet valves to control the flow of steam to the cylinders. Part of the mechanism ran from the middle driving wheel to the angled cylinders. Twenty years after this picture was taken, the engine was subject to further experimentation, when this valve gear was replaced by a different type, designed by Reidinger.
(N Fields)

Leaving Romiley, 1940. Wartime pictures are few and far between. It was generally assumed that anyone taking pictures of trains, etc, was acting against the national interest. Even more unusually, the engine's number is clear. Heading a train of fitted wagons is class 5 4-6-0 5238, it has just passed through the station, and is on its way to Woodley. The three levels of tracks show up well, each with an offset bracket signal protecting its junction. When replaced, they will be placed on the other side of the line they serve. *(K Oldham)*

Original Line to Romiley, 1951.
In pre-DMU days, this is what suburban services looked like. In the capable hands of class C13 4-4-2T 67939 a Manchester London Road to Hayfield stopping train from Woodley heads towards Romiley on 16th July. Lever no 25 (out of 36) would need to be pulled in Romiley Junction signalbox to move the signal arm.
(T Lewis)

Romiley Station, c.1900. This view north shows a modest station, built in 1862 as part of the MS&LR/ MR joint line to Sheffield. That line continues through the station, then through the right hand arch of the bridge in the background, and on to Woodley. Next to arrive was the line through the other arch from Bredbury, while the Cheshire Lines route passes by a sharp curve to the left, immediately behind the signalbox. Hoisted high above the station buildings is a fine bracket signal. Access to the platforms is by a subway with a distinctive glass dome for the steps to the down platform. *(BPC)*

Romiley Station, c.1910. This posed picture has the staff on the up platform – none are female. In the background are the distant signals that mirror the home signals by the signalbox. Gas would be used for lighting the station, and milk churns were still delivered here. The station crosses Stockport Road at this point, hence the girders to the right. It was the development of the Peak Forest Canal at the end of the 18th century that led to the increase in Romiley's population. From 825 in 1801, an extra 600 lived there forty years later. Increased trade and the railways led to it increasing to 2,416 by the time of the 1901 census – it had tripled in 100 years. *(J Ryan Collection)*

Marple viaduct, c.1960. South of Romiley, the line crosses a valley on viaduct no 30, a stone structure some 308 yards long. This spans not only the basin made by the rivers Goyt and Etherow to the east (which join to make the River Mersey to the west) but also the Peak Forest Canal, visible to the right. It too crosses the valley on three arches dating from 1800. Crossing the viaduct is a "Crab" 2-6-0 with a westbound excursion. By the rear coaches are the signals and the signalbox of the junction there. It may well be about to pass down onto the Cheshire Lines for a run to Skelton Junction. *(AC Gilbert)*

Marple Wharf Junction, c.1955.
The 2.50pm from Manchester Central station to Derby comes off the southern end of the viaduct. Having travelled to Heaton Mersey station it would have arrived here via Stockport Tiviot Dale. Missing out only Strines and Nottingham Road, this (almost) all-stations train would arrive at 6.12pm. Serious travellers to Derby would have waited in Manchester until 4pm for the express, arriving 24 minutes earlier, so the slow train would have been held to allow the express to overtake it. Although it normally took a train about six minutes to pass from Rowsley to Darley Dale, the slow

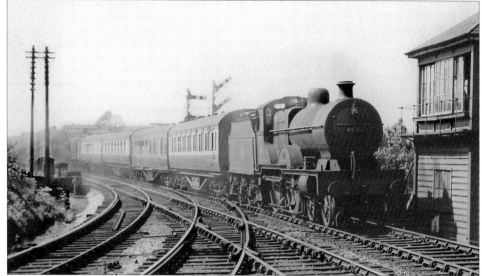

train languished in the up slow line east of Darley Dale station for about thirty minutes. LMS Compound 41118 is of 1925 vintage from Horwich works; it lasted until 1958. *(WA Brown)*

Marple, c.1910. The line through Marple station became a joint MS&LR/MR concern from 1869. Liverpool portions were detached from down trains, and after the departure of the main train to Manchester, an engine that had been waiting in the down bay would back onto the detached portion, and set off for Liverpool. The up arrangements were interesting, for example, the noon express from Liverpool would arrive at the up platform at 1.10pm. It would then pull forward and reverse into the up bay, leaving the coaches there. Meanwhile, at 1pm, the "London Express" would depart from London Road station. On arrival here at 1.15pm, its engine would be detached, pull forward and collect the Liverpool portion from the bay, then reverse them onto the front of the Manchester portion before setting off for the capital. The two companies rebuilt the station in 1875 to give four longer platforms and a lot of passenger protection, as this view south shows. On 2nd August 1880, Manchester Central station was adopted as the place for the division of trains, after which Marple's importance declined. Passengers were spoilt for choice over which Manchester terminus they would end up at, with the joint lines' services going to London Road, and the others to Central. The MR ceased sending passenger trains to London Road from 1884. Goods trains for Manchester used the line in ever increasing numbers, with relief not arriving until 1902 when the Disley cut-off was built. *(J Ryan Collection)*

New Mills Tunnel, 1951. North of Marple, the line hugs one bank of the Goyt valley, while the LNWR line to Buxton hugs the other. With the presence of the Peak Forest Canal this is a very congested place. The train shown has just left the station, which opened on 1st July 1865. It is perched on a ledge with steep rock hills next to the up platform, and a 40ft drop into the river behind the down platform. It has been given the right of way to proceed through the left hand, 197-yard, tunnel (for Hayfield) by the lower-quadrant arms on this impressive bracket signal. The right-hand tunnel is for the main line for Chinley. *(ER Morten)*

New Mills Goods Junction, 1956. North of Marple is a set of goods sidings controlled by this 35-lever MR box, which replaced an earlier one in 1928; the fine bracket signals are for the up goods and the up main line. The goods yard opened some 5 years after the line in 1867, and had capacity for 280 wagons. Half a mile north, New Mills South Junction is reached. Although only a minor coal producing area, New Mills shared the country's doubling of coal production between 1855 and 1875 with the switch to steam power for mills, resulting in an increase in sidings and goods trains. Coal production had doubled again by 1913, and railways were carrying massive quantities as witnessed by the importance of the Glazebrook to Godley line. *(Signalling Record Society, Scrimgeour Collection)*

New Mills South Junction, 1953. In 1865, the Manchester, Sheffield & Lincolnshire Railway built a line to nearby Hayfield, and this section was built by the Midland Railway in 1867 to link that line with their own at New Mills. This allowed access to Manchester from their line at Chinley (from 1867), Derby and the East Midlands. An MR Compound 4-4-0 is hauling a Derby to Manchester stopping train towards New Mills Goods Junction. Marple and Stockport Tiviot Dale will be calling points before the train terminates at Manchester Central. In the foreground are the lines that continue via Disley tunnel to Cheadle Heath. The controlling signalbox is in the distance on the right. *(ER Morten)*

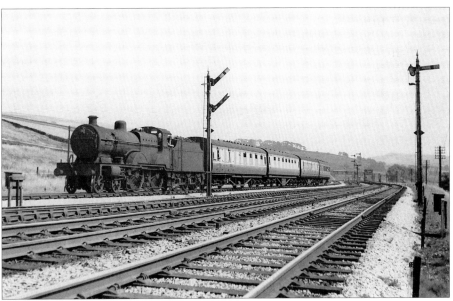

Back on the Glazebrook to Godley line Towards Woodley Station

Woodley Exterior, 1984. Woodley station was opened by the MS&LR and MR when their lines were extended from Hyde to Marple. The station buildings were on the down side, and date from the opening of the line in 1862. They were extended by the addition of a gable on the right on the arrival of the Cheshire Lines the next year. They even had refreshment facilities, as it wasn't until corridor stock became commonplace on longer distance trains that stops for

food and drink were discontinued. As at Romiley, it was the development of the Peak Forest Canal that led to an increasing population, but any passenger trade was soon stolen by the coming of the railways. *(ND Mundy)*

Woodley Station, Looking North, c.1905. A down train is expected judging by the passengers, trolleys and waiting staff, of which there appear to be a fair number. Although the scene is instantly recognizable, even today, there are minor differences. Gone are the milk churns, the gas lights, metal adverts, and the full-stop on station nameboards. Fortunately, the fine lattice footbridge still survives. Hyde Road bridge obscures driver's views of signals, so for both directions they are high in the air, and the down starter also has a repeater at the driver's eye-level. The next bridge along the line, a short road to a mill from Poleacre Lane, was similarly in the way. The bracket signals are for Apethorne junction, which is before the third bridge. The signals and the signalbox on the up platform, to the right, have a fascinating history, and there were originally two brackets,

each with two arms. These signals show that there were three signalboxes in the area. Just under the second bridge on the down side was Woodley (South) box, and the signal just visible was the distant for Woodley (West) box, which was situated round the Cheshire Lines curve just before the Hyde Road bridge. Both boxes went in the 1930s, so later photographs have these arms missing. *(Stations UK)*

Woodley Station, Looking South. Disappearing into the distance under Smithy Green and High Lane bridges is the line to Romiley. Taken from the footbridge, this view shows an up-side waiting shelter with the signalbox at the end of the platform. At this time both home and distant arms were painted red with a white vertical stripe on them. Departing to the right is the line to Bredbury with its 10mph speed limit. *(BPC)*

Woodley Station, 1959. "Engineering works may cause disruption to your journey" was a common quotation. The diverted 2pm Manchester Central to London (St Pancras) passes Woodley hauled by LMS Stanier Jubilee 4-6-0 45622 *Nyasaland* on 12th April. The train had probably arrived here via the Fallowfield loop, Guide Bridge and Hyde, with the capital being reached after an epic journey of over five and a quarter hours (it took almost a hour less on weekdays). Well illustrated is the height (or lack of it) of the platforms. It wasn't until 1990 that the "drop" was reduced. *(Peter Hutchinson)*

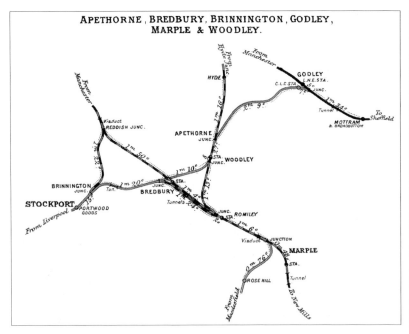

APETHORNE, BREDBURY, BRINNINGTON, GODLEY, MARPLE & WOODLEY.

Woodley Signalbox, c.1955. The diagrams in signalboxes were usually situated on the side facing the traffic. The white dots are bulbs that illuminate when a train is in that section, a low voltage current being passed from one rail to the other due to the metal wheels and axle completing the circuit. The Dutton frame and levers are different from others on the line, although the principle was the same – one couldn't pull or push a lever, until the release mechanism had been pressed. On each of the fifty levers there is a number and description of its purpose. *(Signalling Record Society, Scrimgeour Collection)*

Woodley Station, c.1960. The electrification of the main line to Manchester via Crewe meant that for a time trains had to be diverted by other routes (a very difficult problem today, due to closures). Arriving on the line from Romiley is such an express train being hauled by an unidentified Britannia class 4-6-2 engine. *(J Lloyd)*

Woodley West, 1968. Heading west down the slope is a coal train bound for Heaton Mersey on 15th February. The engine is about to pass over Hyde Road with Mill Lane bridge ahead. Until 6th June 1936, a signalbox was on the other side of the line, but it was replaced by this ground frame, which controlled the entrance to the goods yard by a trailing slip. This arrangement ended in the early 1970s. While both signal posts appear to be of typical Cheshire Lines design, the left-hand arm is a replacement, as it is upper-quadrant, while the one on the right is lower-quadrant. Note the tall signal just visible in the background. *(BPC)*

Woodley Junction, 1965. Stanier 8F 2-8-0 48376 banks a train of pig iron up the gradient from Stockport, the last section being at 1 in 61. The train is leaving the Stockport & Woodley Railway, and passing onto the joint line. By this time, the goods yard had been taken over by a scrap metal merchant who, as with the coal depot, appears to be doing a brisk trade. The adjacent coal yard had the mechanized face of coal distribution before North Sea Gas came on stream. Different hoppers contained different grades of coal ready to be bagged up for sale to customers. A 3-ton crane was in the goods yard. *(John Fairclough)*

Origins and Destinations of Traffic North of Godley

Apethorne Junction, 1965. A third of a mile north of Woodley station is the site of the junction of the line to Godley with the line from Hyde Junction on the Manchester, Sheffield & Lincolnshire Railway main line. Just north of Hyde Junction, near Guide Bridge, were the extensive Dewsnap sidings – probably the origin of this freight train on 31st August. Hauling the fitted train is Stanier 2-6-0 42977. The top signal arm has been pulled off by the adjacent signalbox, Apethorne Junction, but the bottom arm is still on. This was operated by the signalman in the box in front, Woodley. Most probably the train will turn west at Woodley, so its speed would need to be kept low. *(Peter Fitton)*

Apethorne Junction, 1951. LNER 4-4-2T class C13 67422 passes along the original line from Hyde with a train, probably for Hayfield; the mills in Hyde make up the background. This 14-lever box, and its signals, lasted a few months over one hundred years. The down signal's arms have white boards behind them to make them stand out better, the right-hand arm being for Godley, and the other for Hyde. It would be along this line that trains from the Cheshire Lines went to Guide Bridge and Yorkshire via Stalybridge, or to Oldham via the Oldham, Ashton and Guide Bridge Junction Railway. *(CHA Townley)*

Hyde Central Station, Pre-war. This view from the down platform shows the rather lavish station buildings, mostly on the up side. Its awning was removed from all but the far building, and the gas light eventually gave way to electric, although the semaphore signal persisted for some time. Next to the station was the extensive boiler works of Joseph Adamson. *(BPC)*

Hyde North, 1954. Passing through this part of Hyde is the original 1841 Sheffield, Ashton-under-Lyne & Manchester Railway that went on to become MS&LR and then the GCR. When the joint (MS&JR and MR) line was built towards Marple, this station was called Hyde Junction even though it only had platforms on the joint line and none on the main Manchester to Sheffield route. If it had been built 200 yards to the north it could have served both. The buildings across the line belong to Daniel Adamson, boilermaker, and uncle to Joseph who had a works at Hyde Central – a lot of their workers used the station. Entering is a train for Macclesfield from London Road (departure 9.28am SO) with LNER class C13 4-4-2T 67447 preparing to stop. *(HC Casserley)*

Hyde Junction, 1961. Looking west across the main lines between Manchester and Sheffield we see that there were platforms only on the joint line – those with overhead wiring had none. Heading north, towards Dewsnap sidings, is Austerity 2-8-0 90328 on 18th August. When the Hyde bypass (M63) was being built, the line to Romiley was closed, and temporary wooden platforms were set up on the main line. They had narrow platforms due to the cramped nature of the site, and passengers were escorted across the line to the up side by anxious BR staff on a boarded crossing. With the completion of the new concrete railway bridge over the motorway, the temporary station was removed and Hyde North reopened for business. *(E Bentley)*

Dewsnap Sidings, late 1940s. Within a quarter of a mile of Hyde Junction, Dewsnap sidings were encountered. These, together with Godley Junction and some others in the Guide Bridge area, were the main sorting areas for wagons along the Woodhead line. With the building of Mottram yard in 1935, Dewsnap became the focal point for up traffic (that is, towards Sheffield) leaving Mottram for down trains. Waiting in the sidings is LNER 2-8-0 class O4 63710. *(CM Bentley)*

Dewsnap sidings, 1956. The sidings occupy the third of a mile between the Astley Street and Dewsnap bridges to the north of the main line. Before their construction, there was plenty of mining activity in the area around Astley Deep Pit. The sidings consisted of three reception roads and five shunting necks leading to 57 blind-ended sidings in four groups. It had its own signalbox controlling movements in and out of the yard and the up and down goods lines. Most traffic went east, but a small amount went around the curve north to Stalybridge. Taken from the up fast line, this view shows the brick-based GCR 1905 40-lever signalbox well. Trains would draw up to the strange looking signal bracket on one of the reception roads, in front of us, and the engine (steam O4 or electric Bo-Bo) would be detached, and a shunting engine (a J11 or a diesel) would pull the wagons past the box onto one of the five shunting necks to our right. The wagons would then be pushed into the sidings, often more than one train being shunted at a time. The method of dividing a train was extremely crude – the engine would push the wagons (which had been uncoupled in the appropriate place) down the 1 in

77 gradient into the sidings. The "cut" of wagons was pursued by chasers, who applied the brakes. Too soon and the next "cut" would collide, and possibly cause a derailment. Too late and the chaser had a long run after them and a long walk back! In this crude but effective manner a trains were assembled. *(Signalling Record Society, Scrimgeour Collection)*

Guide Bridge East, 1950. What a splendid example of a LNER lattice bracket signal! Heading east along the up goods line is LNER 2-8-0 class O4 63822. Above the tender can just be made out the controlling signalbox. The engine has just passed over the curve from the Stalybridge branch and ahead is Dewsnap sidings. The signal indicates that the train is to pass into one of the two up goods lines that served the sidings. *(HC Casserley)*

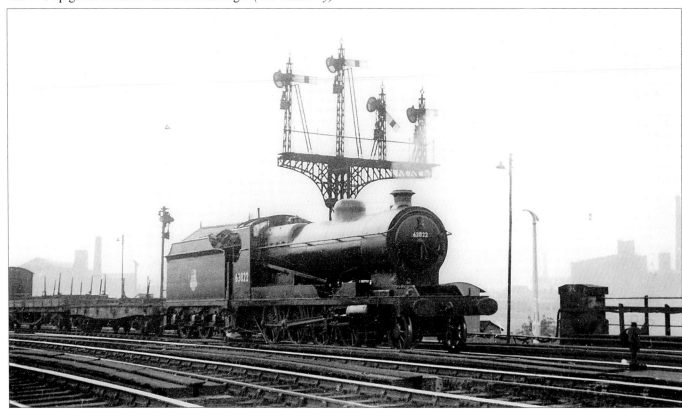

Along the Glazebrook to Godley Line from Woodley

This short 2¼-mile section of line was actually built by the MS&LR from 1863. An interesting feature of the building of the line was that the contractors, Knight & Gordon, were to secure the running lines directly to the sleepers using cast iron brackets bolted through the rails. This saved 19 tons of cast iron per mile, with consequent financial savings. The ownership of this section was transferred to the committee that ran the

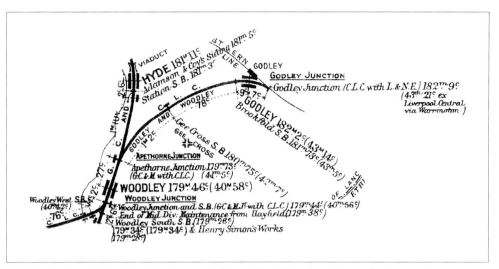

Cheshire Lines on 10th August 1866, just over six months after it had opened for traffic. This short line and others, when put together, made up the Cheshire Lines, which its joint owners used to get goods to the LNWR-dominated Manchester and Liverpool areas. However, odd bits like this had to fit in with existing lines, often causing severe gradients and curves.

Apethorne Junction, 1965. Leaving Cheshire Lines metals, and traversing the roughly ⅓-mile MR/GCR joint line, is a loaded coal train on 31st August. Stanier 8F 2-8-0 48631 is coming down the 1 in 100 gradient, and obeying the 25mph speed limit. Ahead is Woodley station, then after an easterly turn, Cheshire Lines metals can be regained. The signals show up well above the bridge. A train towards Godley is expected, judging by the squat bracket signal post in front of the signalbox. *(Peter Fitton)*

Hyde, 1968. 4th May is a date that will be sadly remembered by many rail enthusiasts. This was the last day of steam workings from Heaton Mersey shed, and this is believed to be the very last one, hence the balloons and wreath. Fittingly, this honour fell to Stanier 8F 2-8-0 48115 doing what had been done a thousand times before – hauling empty mineral wagons east to be refilled. The train has just left Apethorne Junction with the bridge in the background. *(P Hutchinson)*

Hyde, 1958. When the line was first built, several homes in what is now Dowson Road (Swain Street at that time) were demolished. Dowson Road was extended over the line in the 1930s as a relief for Stockport Road. Heading an express train through the cutting here is Standard class 4 76089 on 6th September. Judging by the LNER coaches, it could be a train connecting Yorkshire towns with Welsh coastal resorts, and by running along the Godley to Skelton Junction section, the congestion of Manchester could be avoided. *(Joe Lloyd)*

Peel Street, Hyde, 1966. A train of limestone hoppers is on the up line with a Stanier 8F on the front. Having done its duty, 9F 2-10-0 92024 goes gently down the slope either to be serviced at Heaton Mersey shed or to bank another train from Stockport on 23rd July. Such engines were not rare along the line, and their frequency increased as steam engines were concentrated at the fewer and fewer depots that could service them. Ten engines of this

class were modified to have Crosti boilers, readily identified by the bumps on either side of their smoke box, and instead of the firebox gases being ejected from the chimney, they were passed in the reverse direction through a pre-heater (a secondary boiler) to be ejected from the final chimney on the right hand side near to the cab. This led to visibility problems for footplate crews, and to the strange sight of smoke coming out three quarters of the way along the boiler. Some were fitted with small smoke deflectors. If an indifferent performer had been so modified, the inventor might have got some return for his investment, but as the 9Fs were such good engines anyway, the trials were inconclusive. *(Joe Lloyd)*

Dove House Bridge, 1966. Rounding the curve heading towards Apethorne Junction is a RCTS excursion on 26th March. Now preserved Jubilee 4-6-0 45596 *Bahamas* leads the train with probably every window open and occupied by enthusiasts. The engine has a double chimney now, and the yellow diagonal on the cabside indicated to the footplate crew that the engine was not to run under the overhead wires of the newly-electrified part of the Manchester/ Liverpool to London route. On the left can just be seen the start of the loop and an upper-quadrant signal is just visible over Dove House bridge.
(Peter Fitton)

Dove House Bridge, 1953. About half a mile west of Godley Junction along the Cheshire Lines, the southern part of Hyde is encountered with its deep cuttings and numerous over-bridges, one of which is Dove House. Looking towards Godley, this view shows an unidentified fitted freight nicely framed by the stone bridge. Before 1928, banking engines could push trains from Stockport up the gradient almost to Godley. In the southern part of Hyde there was a crossover and a signalbox at Gee Cross, which may have allowed the bankers to leave their trains and to run back to Stockport. Track circuiting later allowed this intermediate block post to be done away with. *(Joe Lloyd)*

Dove House Bridge, 1953. To cater for the exchange of locomotives at Godley junction after electrification, an up loop was constructed along the Cheshire Lines route. This was quite long (1,640 yards) and stretched from close to Brookfold box to the iron footbridge across the line from Walker Lane. A fine example of a Cheshire Lines lower quadrant home signal, and the almost-completed extension to the bridge, are both clearly seen. *(Joe Lloyd)*

The Cheshire Lines Railway at Godley and its Junctions

Exchange of motive power at Godley, 1968.
After electrification in the early 1950s, Godley Junction was the scene of many locomotive changes at the steam/electric boundary. Having been taken by a steam engine from the colliery to (probably) Wath yard, electric engines would pull them through Woodhead tunnel. Upon arrival here, the train would pass along the down loop where the engine would be uncoupled; it would return east with a train of empties. The train started off at 09.55 from Rotherwood exchange sidings, east of Sheffield, and would have been hauled here by an electric engine. Leaving Godley is a coal train on 10thApril. Stanier 8F 2-8-0 48322 has just been turned, and is heading west along the main line to Apethorne Junction and onto Garston Docks. Ireland, having no fossil fuels of its own is dependent on importing power from the UK. Over such a short distance, this constant change of engines cannot have been cost effective, but perhaps the increased speed of loaded coal trains, and consequent increased capacity on the line, was worth it. Who knows what the effect of the "Grand Plan" (to electrify the Cheshire Lines route to Liverpool, as well as that to Manchester Central) would have been? (The 3rd rail electrified services from Southport to Hunt's Cross are part of this.) *(R Elsdon)*

Leaving Godley, 1968. Stanier 8F 2-8-0 48322 sets off west with coal bound for Garston. In the background can be seen the Hyde factory of Wall's. The premises were used for the manufacture of margarine until about 1921, when Wall's took it over to make ice cream. Boxes of the products were loaded onto goods and express trains for the east coast. During World War II, production switched to meat pies and sausages, with ice cream manufacture heading south to near Gloucester after the War. Kerr Foods now operate from the site, and Wall's products are still made there.
(R Elsdon)

Up Goods at Godley Junction, around 1960. A Wallerscote to Whitemoor train is awaiting acceptance at the starting signals on the right before proceeding into the up branch platform. Trying to get in the picture, to the left of Stanier 8F 2-8-0 48747, is Brookfold signalbox. The signalman would pull lever 37 to lower the top arm, but the lower arm would be operated from the box in front, Godley Junction. Lever 39 would raise the yellow arm with a black chevron on its rear. The signals on the left are for the down main (with a calling on arm underneath), while the two signals on the smaller concrete post control the down loop and its exit onto the down branch. *(Roy Harrison)*

Godley, 1968. Seen earlier leaving Apethorne Junction is 48115, and to complete what is probably the last day of steam working along the route, it is being turned at the 70ft turntable on the down side beyond Brookfold box. In 1940, an enemy bomb just missed this piece of railway equipment, and had it hit, this vital railway artery would have been severed. *(P Hutchinson)*

Shunting at Godley. Wherever there are sidings there will be shunting engines and Godley was no exception – engines of classes N5 and J10/J11 commonly performed this function. A turntable and water column were provided, and originally these were at the end of the Cheshire Lines sidings, where we find *(top)* LNER N5 class 0-6-2T E9328 in early BR years, later to become BR 69328. However, by 1935 the servicing facilities had been moved to the other end by Brookfold signalbox. This is where we find *(bottom)* 0-6-0 J10 5145 (complete with 4,000 gallon tender and original Pollit chimney) in this 1946 photograph. In 1949, it became 65145, lasting until 1958. Locomotive servicing would have been carried out at Heaton Mersey shed, and for other engines, at Gorton. Sidings at Godley and Mottram caused a lot of light engine trips both ways. *(Both, Great Central Railway Society)*

Cheshire Lines Up Platform, 1939. Arriving at Godley at 6.44pm is 4-4-0 5855 with an all-stations (including Widnes Central) train from Liverpool on 1ˢᵗ June. It is likely that similar down trains left from this platform, thereby reducing passenger movements across the line; there was no footbridge connecting the Cheshire Lines island platform to the main ones. *(CA Appleton, collection Bob Miller)*

Godley, 1947. While not the sharpest of pictures, this is included to show traffic not usually photographed. Heading down from Godley Junction on its way (most probably) to Aintree is LNER B17 4-6-0 2861 *Sheffield Wednesday*, the first few vehicles being horse boxes. While passenger trains to the raccs are not uncommon, this vital traffic is rarely seen. Note the practice of using white metal discs in place of lamps to describe the train to railway staff, and the speed limit sign on the left. *(Joe Lloyd)*

Brookfold Signalbox, 1981. This box was situated a short distance from the Stockport end of the up platform. The 41-lever box was wider than most, and with its porch at the top of the stairs and horizontal cladding, was different from other boxes in the area. Long after the demise of steam, motive power changes still took place between electric and diesel locomotives. Its days were numbered when, in 1981, the Woodhead tunnel closed. With it went the trains along the Cheshire Lines route and Brookfold box. Vandals set fire to it in 1982. *(BPC)*

Views from Brookfold Signalbox, 1960s. Taken by signalman Roy Harrison, these three pictures illustrate the importance of this route.

Right: It is 6am, and this train of empties from Glazebrook is on its way past the up branch platform to Godley up sidings where an electric engine will take it forward. The seven sidings (six plus an engineers' siding) had a capacity of 255 wagons. In the middle of the picture is an 08 diesel shunter from Gorton about to perform its duties. These will include bringing the wagons that will form the 5.30am Godley to Liverpool from No 1 sidings, and the 6.55am (6F87) Godley to Widnes West Deviation Junction coal train from No 2 sidings. On the extreme right, No 3 sidings (colloquially known as "Klondike sidings") are full of loaded wagons ready to proceed west at their allotted time.

Bottom right: This shows how trains arriving from the east were organised into one of the dozen blind-ended down sidings. When their departure time approached, a Gorton based 08 diesel shunter would pull them onto the down through siding as shown here. By this time, the station buildings had been largely removed leaving a small building that the yard crew used as a mess hut. Foreman Bill Manifold is to the right of the engine.

Below: With appropriate motive power attached to the front, loaded coal trains would proceed westwards. However, there were also general freight trains passing along the line. Two trains left Mottram yard at 4.05am (6F96) and 4.35am (7H50), and according to Rule 55, were allowed to wait one behind the other on the down through siding until their motive power arrived. In this case it is an unidentified "Crab" 2-6-0.

Godley Junction, undated. Godley station was one of the original stations on the Sheffield, Ashton under Lyne & Manchester Railway, but lasted only a year until 1842. The junction station came into being nearly 25 years after the original station closed, when the same company opened a line from Woodley to join the main line here on 1st February 1866. This section was transferred to the Cheshire Lines on 10th August the same year. Although the nameboard is partially hidden, it tells a story. The GCR decided that this was a junction "for Liverpool", and from 1910, a handful of trains from Sheffield stopped here, enabling passengers to proceed west without having to go into Manchester with a probable change of termini. After World War II, these connections had gone. This view shows just a handful of the staff at the time. *(Tameside Local Studies & Archive)*

Looking North, 1909. This superb view shows the junction in all its glory. The main line towards Manchester curves away to the right, with the Woodley line off to the left. The station buildings have an extensive canopy around them. The signalbox was not yet at the up end of the up main platform – this did not happen until later. Some 6-wheel coaches are in the up, "Sand Pit", sidings. While gas lights were provided on the island platform, they were probably little used as both up and down trains used the down face of the canopied platform. As this didn't involve crossing the line on foot, it was probably safer. *(J Ryan Collection)*

Godley Junction, undated. *Top:* The station consisted of up and down platforms on both main and branch lines, with the down main and the up branch lines forming a "V". The station buildings were situated where the platforms met, and there was a single booking office in the apex of the block. The waiting rooms and other facilities were duplicated on the Cheshire Lines side (on the left) and the MS&LR side (on the right), and were staffed by personnel with the insignia of their respective companies. The railway workers from each company had separate accommodation too, and this rivalry persisted between the Cheshire Lines and LNER until nationalization in 1948, when the joint company lost its identity.

Middle: A once-covered footbridge led to a small wooden shelter on the up main platform, with the junction signalbox beyond.

Bottom: The down island platform was devoid of anything, apart from gas lights, and it never had a footbridge, which made access to it extremely hazardous. With few passenger trains, the small number of passengers would be escorted across the line by railway staff, but today's health and safety environment would make this impossible.

Hull to Liverpool and Manchester Services, 1939. Every afternoon, just after tea, the following scene was enacted. A train to the two Lancashire cities set off as one from Hull at 2.45pm. It would arrive at the Cheshire Lines island platform at Godley Junction at 5.35pm, and the last two coaches would be detached from the rest of the train. The front portion would then go forward at 5.39pm to Liverpool Central (arriving at 6.47pm) stopping at Stockport Tiviot Dale and Warrington Central on the way. A shunting engine, often an N5 0-6-2T like E9328 seen earlier, would be waiting in the Cheshire Lines sidings to back onto the two coaches, and pull them back onto the down main line where they would be pushed into the ex-GCR down main platform. Waiting there would be an engine to take them (at 5.42pm) to Manchester London Road to arrive 5.58pm. On 1st June, it was the duty of almost brand-new LNER V2 2-6-2 4828 to do this short trip. Later, it would take the 6.31pm Manchester to Sheffield train, and would therefore be tender-first for the short journey from Godley. Liverpool to Hull workings went via Manchester Central and the Fairfield loop: the reverse of the working described here would have been extremely difficult. As an added complication, a Hull-Sheffield-Liverpool (but not Manchester) working in the early 1930s would pass Godley and go via the Fairfield loop line. On reaching Throstle Nest Curve, the train joined the main Cheshire Lines route to Liverpool, and so avoided Manchester. *(CA Appleton)*

NOTICE
PURSUANT TO THE PROVISIONS OF THE ACT OF PARLIAMENT 24 AND 25 VIC CAP 70 THE CHESHIRE LINES COMMITTEE BEING LIABLE FOR THE REPAIR OF THIS BRIDGE HEREBY GIVE NOTICE THAT THE SAME IS INSUFFICIENT TO CARRY WEIGHTS BEYOND THE ORDINARY TRAFFIC OF THE DISTRICT AND PARTICULARLY THAT IT IS INSUFFICIENT FOR THE CARRIAGE OF TRACTION OR OTHER LOCOMOTIVE ENGINES DRAWING PROPELLING OR CARRYING AN EXCESSIVE WEIGHT WITHIN THE MEANING OF THE HIGHWAYS AND LOCOMOTIVES AMENDMENT ACT 1878 AS AMENDED BY THE LOCOMOTIVES ACT 1898
BY ORDER

Opposite page, bottom: **Godley Junction, 1952.** Stopping next to the long wooden shelter on the up main platform is a train for Glossop. Typical of such services was LNER class C13 4-4-2 67431 with three non-corridor coaches, the journey taking around 45 minutes. After stopping at Glossop, the push-pull nature of the service enabled it to reverse and continue to Hadfield. Electrification would bring a fleet of eight, 3-car multiple units, offering almost twice as many trains per day with a half-hourly service. *(J Davenport, Initial Photographics)*

Opposite page, top: **Passing Godley Signalbox, c.1960.** A down express passes the 44-lever signalbox on the down main line heading for Manchester. LNER class B1 4-6-0 61011 *Waterbuck* is passing over the junction of the Cheshire Lines west to Woodley; the sidings to the right seem to be busy. An electric engine is on the up main line in the distance. At this point the lines are quadruple, and would be so for just over ½ mile to Godley East Junction. *(Great Central Railway Society)*

Origins and Destinations of Traffic East of Godley

Two deep valleys dominate the landscape to the east of Godley. One was made by the River Etherow and the other was across Dinting Vale. Between the two, the LNER built its Mottram marshalling yard to sort traffic for the subsequent parting of the ways at Godley for destinations north (to eastern Manchester) or east (to Cheshire, western Manchester and Liverpool).

Godley East, 1954. Moving its westbound fitted freight train from the down main to the down loop is LNER O4 class 2-8-0 63721 *(right)*. Soon after this picture was taken

(in May) such trains would be electrically hauled. To the rear is the controlling signalbox, the 30-lever Godley East Junction. *(J Davenport, Initial Photographics)*

Meanwhile *(below)* heading east up the 1 in 482 gradient, is sister engine 63724 – note the variety of wagons it is pulling. The headlamp code denotes, "through mineral or empty wagon train". The signal arm above the tender is for the up goods as it coalesces with the line our train is on – the up main. *(BKB Green)*

Godley East 1969.
These superb views of the all-wooden box were taken from an up train. Ahead is the colour light with its arm signifying the start of the quadruple section to Godley Junction. With the falling off of traffic, the tracks were reduced to two and were separated so that in the space created, an island platform could be opened on 8th May 1978. The halt, called Hattersley, was staffed by a booking clerk.
(MA King)

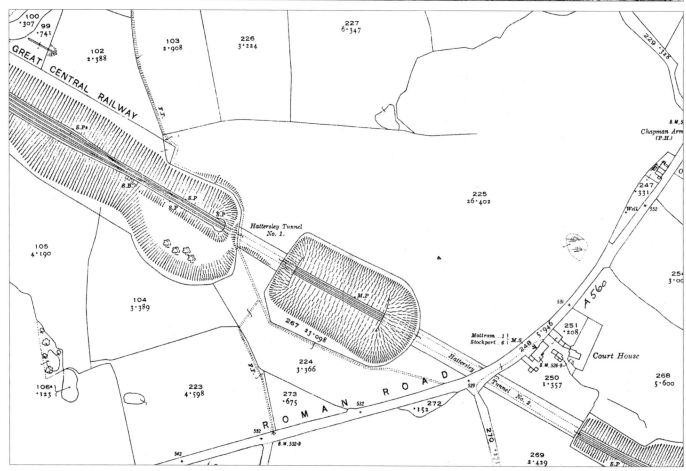

Opposite page: **Hattersley Tunnels, 1930.** When the line first opened in the 1840s, there was a tunnel between Godley and Broadbottom. However, the removal of a portion affected by ground movement resulted in two tunnels separated by a cutting. The shorter No 1 tunnel (96yd) was separated by a 120yd deep cutting from No 2 tunnel (262yd), which carried the Mottram Old Road and Stockport Road over the line. Over time, the instability of the ground became so bad that the gap between up and down trains became critical. The only real solution, bearing in mind that the line was a candidate for quadrupling, was to remove the tunnels completely, and this happened between 1928 and 31. Looking east, we see the two tunnels ready for demolition and the extent of the necessary earth works. On the left are temporary main lines, while the contractor's lines are on the right. The bracket signal is for Godley East. *(Photo: BPC. Map reproduced by kind permission of the Ordnance Survey)*

East of Godley, 1951. A superb picture of a train in the cutting where the tunnels use to be. This view nicely illustrates one of the many coal trains that traversed the route, and continued down along the Cheshire Lines to the docks at Liverpool. LNER class O4/8 2-8-0 63862 heads west on 28th July. Although the supports have been erected, there are no overhead wires yet. *(BWL Brooksbank)*

Broadbottom, c.1941. An up train of coal empties is double-headed by a Q7 0-8-0 piloting a Raven Q6 0-8-0 as it passes under the iron bridge towards Mottram station (visible underneath). Both engines have a tarpaulin rolled and tied back on the cab roof. This would be unrolled at night to prevent any glare from the firebox being detected by enemy aeroplanes. Up to 1935, the sorting of goods trains on the western side of the Woodhead tunnel was done in sidings at Dewsnap, Guide Bridge and Godley Junction, with Dewsnap concentrating on the west to east movements. Not only were the other sidings inadequate, but their connections necessitated crossing the main lines, so opportunities for timings to go awry were rife. Also, due to the inadequate nature of the sidings, they were very slow to deal with trains, causing them to stack up while they were waiting to be dealt with. *(Kenneth Oldham)*

Mottram and Broadbottom Station, around 1900. This view is looking west from the end of the low up platform, as a train from Manchester approaches. We are standing on the trailing single-slip crossover to the goods yard, which consisted of a shed, a loading dock and a coal siding – the stop block is at the end of the latter. Opening on 10th December 1842 as Broadbottom, this simple country station is still open for business, with its fine iron footbridge and nicely proportioned road bridge. In 1884, it took the name shown here, only to lose the Mottram part in 1954. Now that the lines have been electrified, the footbridge has been partly boarded-up for safety reasons. *(Stations UK)*

Mottram Marshalling Yard

In 1935, the LNER built a yard on the flattish ground between the Dinting Arches (Mottram Viaduct) and the next viaduct over the River Etherow to sort wagons destined west of Woodhead. It was designed to handle 700 to 1,000 wagons per shift, depending on their method of coupling. The traffic originated at collieries in Yorkshire, Derbyshire and Nottinghamshire, and there was also steel from Sheffield and materials from the eastern counties. After sorting at Mottram, trains were forwarded to parts of Lancashire, Liverpool docks, and Shotton steelworks in North Wales. Its construction was complicated by the geology of the area, and although over 1¼ million cubic yards of material were removed to make the cutting, it was mostly tipped as spoil at the side of the line. Only a quarter of this was used to create embankments, with the addition of a 20ft thickness of ash. Areas of the embankments had silt on top of rock, and as this would have moved with the increased weight on top, sheet piling was put in down to solid rock. Behind the piles at the toe of the embankments, 20ft-thick retaining walls of concrete were built. Glossop Road almost divided the site in half, and it was originally carried on five stone arches over the two running lines. Three of these were retained, and three new brick arches were built. Separating the two sets of arches was an 80ft long steel girder bridge. The main line was diverted under the third original stone arch, while the roads connecting the two parts of the yard passed under the steel span some 55ft above them.

Reception, 1957. This was taken from Glossop Road bridge looking towards Dinting, and shows the reception sidings; it gives some idea of the amount of land that was removed to create the yard. A long electrically-hauled express passenger train speeds past on the up main line. Since 1954, trains were hauled by class EM1 Bo-Bo electric locomotives, but prior to this, GCR O4s were the mainstay of the cross-Pennine services. The engine would run light to the western end of the yard to take a train forward, or proceed light-engine to its next turn at Godley, Dewsnap or Gorton shed. *(D Chatfield)*

Sorting, 1946. Turning round to look the other way in this view of the sorting loops, we see an unidentified 2-8-0 working hard with an up freight along the main line. A worker's halt would soon be built on the main line near to where the engine is. There are at least four engines working in the yard judging by the plumes of smoke. On the left is the yard box, with the king point next to it. This controlled which loop the wagons were to be sent to, so that trains were not only divided, but new ones were built up ready for their easterly departure. *(K Oldham)*

Mottram Sidings, 1954. This shot was taken on the last day that steam-hauled passenger trains traversed the whole of the Woodhead route. The next day traffic was suspended through the tunnel, and for the next three months steam and electric passenger trains changed over at Penistone. Freight trains were now electrically hauled to Mottram, Godley, Guide Bridge and Ashton Moss. Passing Mottram No 2 box on its way to Manchester is LNER class K3 2-6-0 61910 on 12th June. *(Ray Hinton)*

No 1 Box, 1969. After a train had been made up, an engine was coupled to the front to take it west. This box controlled departures from the yard and was externally identical to box No 2 at the other end, apart from the repaired bargeboard. Internally, it had 25 levers (five fewer than No 2) to control the main line and, some distance away, Broadbottom for Mottram Station. *(MA King)*